How to Turn a School Around

Series Editors:
John T. Greer
Donn W. Gresso

Principals Taking
ACTION
Series

Joint publications of
THE NATIONAL ASSOCIATION OF SECONDARY SCHOOL PRINCIPALS
and
CORWIN PRESS, INC.

Rethinking Student Discipline
Alternatives That Work
Paula M. Short, Rick Jay Short, and Charlie Blanton

Thriving on Stress for Success
Walter H. Gmelch and Wilbert Chan

Creating Safe Schools
What Principals Can Do
Marie Somers Hill and Frank W. Hill

Quality Teaching Through Professional Development
Allan A. Glatthorn and Linda E. Fox

Creating Better Schools
What Authentic Principals Do
Louise L. MacKay and Elizabeth Welch Ralston

How to Turn a School Around
What Principals Can Do
Anna L. Valdez Perez, Mike M. Milstein, Carolyn J. Wood,
and David Jacquez

Anna L. Valdez Perez
Mike M. Milstein
Carolyn J. Wood
David Jacquez

How to Turn a School Around

What Principals Can Do

CORWIN PRESS, INC.
A Sage Publications Company
Thousand Oaks, California

For information address:

Corwin Press, Inc.
A Sage Publications Company
2455 Teller Road
Thousand Oaks, California 91320
E-mail: order@corwinpress.com

SAGE Publications Ltd.
6 Bonhill Street
London EC2A 4PU
United Kingdom

SAGE Publications India Pvt. Ltd.
M-32 Market
Greater Kailash I
New Delhi 110 048 India

Printed in the United States of America

Library of Congress Cataloging-in-Publication Data

Main entry under title:
    How to turn a school around: What principals can do /
by Anna L. Valdez Perez, . . . [et al.].
        p. cm.—(Principals taking action)
    Includes bibliographical references.
    ISBN 0-8039-6663-6 (cloth: acid-free paper)
    ISBN 0-8039-6664-4 (pbk.: acid-free paper)
    1. School improvement programs—United States. I. Valdez Perez,
Anna L. II. Series: Principals taking action series.
LB2822.82 .H695 1999
371.2'00973—dc21   98-40270

99 00 01 02 03 04 05 7 6 5 4 3 2 1

Corwin Editorial Assistant:	Kristen L. Gibson
Production Editor:	Denise Santoyo
Editorial Assistant:	Nevair Kabakian
Typesetter:	Lynn Miyata
Cover Designer:	Michelle Lee

Contents

Foreword	vii
Preface	xiii
Organization of the Book	xiv
About the Authors	xv
1. Insights From Literature	**1**
Chapter Focus	1
School Renewal, Reform, and Restructuring	1
Cultural Change	4
Vision Building	5
Facilitative or Transformational Leadership	6
Professional Development Opportunities	9
Support	11
Site-Based Management	12
Summary	14
Notes	14
2. Setting Direction	**15**
Chapter Focus	15
Key Insights From the Literature About Vision and Mission	15
A Visioning Approach	18
The Faculty's Role in Establishing a Vision	19
The Faculty's Role in Establishing a Mission	20
Goal Setting	22

Developing an Action Plan   22
Summary   24

3. **Professional Development**   **25**
Chapter Focus   25
Key Insights From the Literature About
    Professional Development   25
Finding the Resources to Provide
    Professional Development   28
Delivering Professional Development   33
Summary   40

4. **Involving Teachers, Students, and Community
   in Decision Making**   **42**
Chapter Focus   42
Key Insights From the Literature About
    Shared Decision Making   42
Shared Decision Making in Schools   45
Summary   58

5. **Support for Change**   **59**
Chapter Focus   59
Key Insights From the Literature About
    Support for Change   60
Internal Support for Change   61
External Support for Change   65
Summary   69

6. **Synthesis and Transferable Lessons**   **70**
Chapter Focus   70
Key Elements in Systemic Change   71
Putting It All Together   79
In Closing   85

Appendix: The Nine Common Principles of the
    Coalition of Essential Schools   87

References   89

Foreword

Lessons From the Past on
How to Turn a School Around

R eading the manuscript *How to Turn a School Around*, I immediately flashed on another book published almost 40 years ago: Herb Thelen's *Education and the Human Quest* (1960). I remembered it as a remarkable book about change in schools, and even more remarkably I found it on our bookshelves. Herb Thelen was one of my early intellectual gurus; he was Professor of Education at the University of Chicago, conducted research on groups at the National Training Laboratories (NTL) in Bethel, Maine; and he published one of the first books on group dynamics (Thelen, 1954). I spent many summers in the early 1960s with my husband, Dick, learning the principles of group dynamics from wonderful teachers such as Ron Lippitt, Peggy Lippitt, Joe Luft, and other figures in the emerging T-group (training group) sensitivity movement. There was a strong commitment for people to become skilled in group dynamics to bring about moral social change using principles of effective communication, understanding of others, and democratic procedures. Thelen understood much about school change. The authors of *How to Turn a School Around* have the advantage of 40 years of research and best practice to build on as they describe school change efforts.

Thelen promulgated the "School Burning Theory of Education" as one approach to educational change. Of course, he had three other theories that were more reasonable, but after all these years, the burning theory is the one I remembered and that led me back to his book. Thelen (1960) described a school not unlike the school described by Perez, Milstein, Wood, and Jacquez in this text:

> Imagine a perfectly terrible school. The morale of the faculty is scraping bottom; the students are cliquish and many of them don't even speak to each other . . . the citizens are apathetic, depressed and bored. Now comes Rudolph the Brand-new Schoolman with an Idea; school is part of life, and life just doesn't have to be that way. (p. 4)

And Rudolph the Brand-new Schoolman used his ideas and created a wonderful school with all participants involved—the faculty was so successful that some moved on to "spread the gospel," and new teachers flock to this wonderful school; the students excel academically and are active in student government and participate in clubs; the school "converts bullies and terrors from the grammar school into true believers"; parents have "purposive ambition," and "the town swells with pride."

In *How to Turn a School Around: What Principals Can Do*, Principal David French, like Rudolph, the Brand-new Schoolman, doesn't think school life has to be miserable, so he works on changing it. With the help of Ted Sizer's Coalition of Essential Schools, he works with faculty, students, parents, and community to change the "miserable" school into a good place to be. It becomes a good school. After 4 years, David French leaves, and Les Harry becomes the principal and is "committed to the pursuit of continuing improvement." Unfortunately, in the small-town high schools we visited on our tour of 25 districts in 21 states, we never saw a good high school; there were no Rudolphs or Davids to turn a miserable school around (Schmuck & Schmuck, 1992). This book can help school administrators and teachers turn a school around; it summarizes well the literature on school change, which has its roots in the early group dynamics movement.

But, when a school has become "good," this is where you must beware! Be careful! This is where the "School Burning Theory of Education" comes in. Thelen describes Rudolph's school some years later:

> Faculty meetings begin to peter out because nobody seems to have anything to talk about . . . student clubs lose their zip . . . vandalism begins to appear in nasty little ways around the school, and it seems to Rudolph (who has developed a paunch), that the 'good' families have moved away and students aren't what they used to be. . . . The golden age has passed. (pp. 5-6)

> The only thing to do now is set fire to the school, plow up the gardens, retire Rudolph, and start over. Except that this should have been done, right after "and nobody can think of anything further to want." (Thelen, 1960, p. 6)

School change requires continuity; what was an innovation must become institutionalized to prevent backsliding. The effort toward becoming a good school must be a continuous process.

Today, we know a lot more about good practice, technique, skills needed, and have a research base to create a better school than Herb Thelen did in 1960. However, the fact is that there is no technology, no good practice, no technique that can rival the universal quest for human understanding. Thelen knew that in 1960 and it remains true today.

> We must seek . . . an education that seeks, fosters, and builds on the universal human question; an education that believes man should be master, not slave, to his own inventions; an education guided by unattainable values, creating its own procedures from insights which reflect detailed knowledge of boys and girls, communities, and worlds without number. In short—an education. (p. 10)

What does he mean, "unattainable values"? I like it to mean we teach about: communication (written, oral, technological); human expression (art, literature, music); human development (biology, psychology, literature); and about the environment we live in (botany, zoology, sociology, ecology).

What does he mean, "creating its own procedures from insight"? I like it to mean a school that is not steeped in its own bureaucracy; one that continually collects data on its own procedures and uses the data formatively to ask questions about whether its processes work for students. It is a school that knows it will never achieve the Promised Land but continually changes as the forces within and without the school change.

Who helps bring about a good school? Certainly the principal is critical and this book is written primarily for school administrators. But, as the authors point out, it is also the concerted effort among principals, teachers, staff, parents, students, and community that makes a good school. In the 1960s, Rudolph got tired. I think Rudolph didn't have much support from the administrative textbooks or the administrative classes he took in 1960. In 1960, the literature on school administration extolled the works and phrases from classical scientific management—span of control, division of labor, hierarchy, and control. Rudolph was a pioneer!

Over my ensuing years, from the 1960s in the pastoral and energizing climate of NTL, there have been changes in educational administration. It has moved from a top-down, bossing mentality to one that is facilitative and empowering. I think it is not a coincidence that literature on school administration has changed with the advent of feminist scholarship and of the presence of women administrators. While I do not promote an essentialist view that women behave one way and men behave another way, I do believe that women and men in our culture grow up in different realities, learn different lessons, and bring these differences to the administration of schools. Today, we are valuing in administration traits that have been previously stereotyped as "feminine": nurturing, caring, listening, hearing all points of view (Dunlap & Schmuck, 1995). These are the characteristics of both women and men who are successful as school leaders.

One of the pleasures of living a long life is being able to see the paths traveled; it's nice to be old enough to remember the words of

Herb Thelen and to apply those words to schools today. Like the Holy Grail, the quest for human understanding is illusive; but as educators we have no choice but to continue the search. Changing schools is hard work. Perez, Milstein, Wood, and Jacquez know this very well in 1998.

Patricia A. Schmuck
Senior Scholar
Lewis and Clark College
Portland, Oregon

Organization of the Book

The book is organized to help principals and other administrators to improve schools. The book addresses how to develop a collective vision, provide professional development, involve stakeholders in decision making, and elicit support for change. Each chapter presents, and draws lessons from, different aspects of school transformation, examining the particular aspect from a closer vantage point. Within each chapter, applications to an actual change effort will be presented. The first chapter provides a review of the recent literature focused on reform efforts carried out at all levels of education. Chapter 2 focuses on setting the direction for change and on the important activities of defining purposes, missions, visions, and goals.

Chapter 3 examines the contributions of professional development to achieving change by creating a "community of learners." Chapter 4 describes how teachers, students, administration, and community members can learn to collaborate and participate more effectively in decision-making efforts. Chapter 5 looks at support systems and their impact on sustaining school change. Finally, Chapter 6 synthesizes what has been explained to provide further clarity about how schools can be turned around.

Many of the examples in the book are drawn from "Kennedy High School" in "High Point District" (fictitious names), a school that could be anywhere in the United States. Kennedy's experiences with educational change will often be used to illustrate the critical components of turning a school around. When the principal, David French, arrived at Kennedy, he found a school in trouble, and the problems he saw were much worse than the Superintendent described to him in his interview. At Kennedy High School, tardy bells went unheeded, student fights were commonplace, suspensions occurred daily, and teachers and students alike shared negative attitudes. The principal wanted to make a difference. During his time at Kennedy, he encouraged changes in teacher attitudes and student learning marked the beginning of ongoing reform at Kennedy High. David French left Kennedy after his fourth year at the school, but the changes that began during his principalship continue. Les Harry, the school's newest principal, began his term in 1997-1998. Principal Harry acknowledges Kennedy High's past struggles, appreciates the school's current status, and is actively committed to the pursuit of continuing improvement.

About the Authors

Anna L. Valdez Perez is Deputy Superintendent of the Cobre Consolidated Schools and Adjunct Professor at Western New Mexico University. Prior to this position, she was Superintendent of the Carlsbad Municipal Schools in New Mexico. She began her professional career as a bilingual instructional assistant in the Fort Worth Independent School District in Texas, working her way through the ranks for 21 years in the inner-city, multicultural school system. Positions included teacher, human relations trainer, principal, project coordinator, and assistant director of elementary schools. With her experiences in urban and rural schools, she has served as a consultant and facilitator for school improvement in over 60 schools. She received her EdD from the University of New Mexico in 1996. She has a BA and MEd from Texas Christian University. She has published several professional articles, and has taken additional graduate work at Texas Woman's University, Trinity College (Washington, DC), and the Universidad de Salamanca in Spain.

Mike M. Milstein is Professor of Educational Administration at the University of New Mexico. Prior to this position, he was Professor of Educational Administration at SUNY/Buffalo. His teaching, research, and writing interests are in the areas of resiliency, organizational change, and organizational development. He has been actively engaged in school restructuring, with a special interest in educator plateauing and resilience; has facilitated urban school district restructuring teams; provided guidance for rural school district administrative teams; and helped many schools develop structures, modify roles, and learn the necessary skills for effective school restructuring. He received a PhD from the University of California, Berkeley, and has a BA and MA from the University of Minnesota.

Carolyn J. Wood is Professor of Educational Administration at the University of New Mexico. She is also Director of the Center for Technology and Education, as well as the facilitator for the New Mexico Teacher Learning Community, a project funded by an Eisenhower Federal Activities Program grant from the Office of Educational Research and Improvement. She received a PhD from Washington University (St. Louis, MO) in Educational Policy and Administration. Her teaching and research focus is on transformational leadership, participatory decision making, and most particularly on how institutions teach helplessness and the ways individuals succumb to and/or unlearn helplessness. She has created multimedia presentations focused on helplessness and resourcefulness as well as worked with school districts on these topics.

David Jacquez is Assistant Principal at Gadsden High in Anthony, New Mexico. He received most of his leadership training through the National Education Association during his 18 years as a teacher. His teaching experience has been at the middle school level. He was an elementary principal in the Silver City Public Schools and high school principal in the Cobre Consolidated Schools. He is currently working on a second master's degree in theology through Loyola University. He received his MA in administration and BA in education from Western New Mexico University.

Insights From Literature

Chapter Focus

Chapter 1 encompasses discussions of key elements in school transformation as presented in recent literature. The first section provides a general overview of literature relating to school renewal, restructuring, and reform. The sections that follow look at the specific ingredients that researchers and others agree are critical to successful school transformation: cultural change, vision building, leadership, professional development, support, and site-based management.

School Renewal, Reform, and Restructuring

The age-old question of how to turn a school around has received different answers:

1. *Fix the parts*—Improve the school by adopting a proven and innovative educational practice, for example, a new reading or science curriculum.

2. *Fix the people*—Improve the school by providing better professional development opportunities for faculty, for example, more effective inservice training or better preservice preparation.

3. *Fix the school*—Improve the school by assisting school people to solve their own problems more effectively, for example, use an organizational development approach of identifying the problems, diagnosing the causes, and designing and implementing solutions to those problems.

4. *Fix the system*—Improve the school by changing the culture of the district through systemic reform. (Sashkin & Egermeier, 1992)

The emphasis of this schema on "fixing" various entities may help identify where to begin a change effort; however, it is unlikely to result in long-term, systemic change. "Fix-it" approaches tend to rely on an omniscient "fixer" (principal, superintendent, or other agent of change) who knows the nature of each required fix and can swoop down and accomplish it in short, efficient order. The reality of restructuring and reform is rarely so simple. No matter how necessary, without other kinds of accompanying change, implementing new programs and other "fixes" tends not to be sufficient to bring about major school improvement.

Several authors refer to how restructuring and reform actually occur in schools in terms designed to heighten the contrast between the oversimplification of "fixing" and the reality of school reform. Conley (1997) calls the process "incrementalism." Tyack and Cuban (1995) call it "tinkering toward utopia." Kirst (1991) refers to it as "projectitis." Each of these authors indicates that a new school program tends to become known as THE "restructuring project." When the program is implemented, the school is considered to be "restructured"; but in reality, restructuring has not occurred.[1]

Like Conley, Tyack and Cuban, and Kirst, authors Cawelti (1997), Charters and Jones (1973), Corcoran and Goertz (1995), Elmore (1995), Lee and Smith (1994), McLaughlin (1990), and Newmann (1993) also recognize that structural changes often fail to result in reform. Change may take place, but it falls short of producing the advancements in teaching practices that would lead to true reform, that is, improvement in student learning and performance.

Recent literature (Cawelti, 1997; Cohen, 1995; National Association of Secondary School Principals, 1996) consistently calls for systemic rather than incremental change. The National Association of Secondary School Principals' (NASSP) three mandates for successful high school reform, for example, require system-wide enactment and support:

1. Those aspects that are central to teaching and learning must serve as the focus of reform (i.e., the curriculum, instructional strategies, the school environment, use of technology as a learning tool, use of time, as well as assessment and accountability).
2. A web of support (i.e., professional development, diversity, governance, resources, ties to higher education and relationships) must reinforce teaching and learning elements.
3. Leadership must be diffused throughout the school community. (National Association of Secondary School Principals [NASSP], 1996)

Conley's 12 dimensions of restructuring likewise rely on systemic development, application, and implementation for success. Conley (1997) groups the dimensions into three subsets:

Central variables
1. Learning standards
2. Curriculum
3. Instruction
4. Assessment

Enabling variables
5. Learning environment
6. Technology
7. School-community relationships
8. Teaching and learning time

Supporting variables
9. Governance
10. Teacher and principal leadership
11. Personnel structures
12. Contractual relationships

Cawelti (1997) proposes a systemic approach to reform and indicates that attempts at reform and restructuring might better begin with changing attitudes and norms than with organizational structures:

> Teachers might actually learn to teach differently and develop shared expectations and beliefs about what good teaching is, and then invent the organizational structures that go with those shared skills, expectations and beliefs. (p. 11)

School change as perceived today depends on more than creating new programs and structures. As Conley, the National Association of Secondary School Principals, Cawelti, and others conclude, it is necessary to create new images of what schooling should be like and to redefine what educators must do to turn these images into realities.

Some of the most frequently cited elements for inclusion are: (a) *cultural changes,* (b) *vision building,* (c) *the exercise of facilitative or transformational leadership,* (d) *professional development opportunities,* (e) *support,* and (f) *site-based management.* A brief discussion of these six elements follows.

Cultural Change

School culture has been variously defined (see Boyd, 1992; Schein, 1985). Culture includes:

- The *attitudes and beliefs* held by people within and outside of the school
- The *norms* of the school
- The *relationships* between and among individuals and groups (i.e., students, teachers, administrators, parents, community members)

Simply stated, "culture can be defined as: the way we do business around here" (Patterson, Purkey, & Parker, 1986). Several authors (Cawelti, 1997; Conley, 1997; Cohen, 1995; Elmore, 1995; Krug, 1992) acknowledge the power of mental images and mind-sets in shaping school culture and enabling or obstructing school transformation. "Over time," Conley (1997) writes,

> the powerful mental images people have regarding education may cause even the most radical attempts at restructuring to begin to resemble traditional beliefs and practices. (p. 110)

> In many respects restructuring is not primarily the process of establishing new programs, but of developing a new picture . . . of what schooling should look like and what educators should be attempting to achieve. (p. 427)

Cohen (1995) and Cawelti (1997) both suggest strong links between achieving a positive mind-set and the ability to effect change. For Cawelti (1997), as stated earlier, effective structural changes originate in changed attitudes and norms. Similarly, Cohen (1995) observes that individuals may possess content knowledge and technical skills, but without a positive mind-set they are unlikely to achieve successful restructuring.

The literature suggests that changing school culture, with implications for turning around a school that is not performing well, may mean moving from one culture to another. For example, it may mean moving from bureaucracy to community, from isolation to collaboration, or from a teaching orientation to a learning orientation. It also suggests that to be effective, cultural change must begin with or be accompanied by changes in individual mind-sets and outlooks.

Vision Building

Piecemeal or incremental change often occurs when school administrators and faculty adopt structures or techniques because they represent the latest in educational trends. But, adopting an innovation without considering how it will affect other aspects of the organization can compound rather than solve a school's problems. To be effective structures and techniques, such site-based management or block scheduling, must constitute a facet of a coherent whole.

A mental picture or vision can serve to guide school people to coherent change. A vision includes strategies for obtaining the desired outcome and provides a picture of what schooling should look like (i.e., its content) and how educators can recreate or process this mental picture in real life. Nanus (1992) defines an effective vision as comprising five characteristics:

1. It attracts commitment while energizing and motivating people.

2. It creates meaning in people's lives.

3. It establishes a standard of excellence.

4. It provides a picture of what the future should be.

5. It transcends the status quo.

Many students of educational change (Beer, Eisenstat, & Spector, 1990; Boyd, 1992; Conley, 1997; Fullan, 1993b; Hord, 1992; Nanus, 1992) find that the likelihood for successful restructuring and reform efforts increases when educators, students, parents, and community members create and share a common vision. To be effective, the vision must be stated clearly, articulated frequently, and used consistently to guide resource allocation and other decisions made regarding the school. In this manner, a co-created vision can provide an "internal compass" (Conley, 1997) for those involved in making change and assist them in relating individual contributions to the overall goals of reform.

Facilitative or Transformational Leadership

A Greek myth tells of an image asleep in a block of marble; it is carefully brought to life by a sculptor named Pygmalion.[2] George Bernard Shaw borrows from this theme in his play *Pygmalion* (the basis for the musical hit, *My Fair Lady*). Both the myth and the play have been interpreted to mean that one person's expectation of another person's behavior can be a self-fulfilling prophecy (Rosenthal & Jacobson, 1968).

You see, really and truly, apart from the things anyone can pick up (the dressing and the proper way of speaking, and so on), the difference between a lady and a flower girl is not how she behaves, but how she's treated. I shall always be a flower girl to Professor Higgins, because he always treats me as a flower girl, and always will; but I know I can be a lady to you, because you always treat me as a lady, and always will. (Eliza Doolittle in *Pygmalion* by George Bernard Shaw)

Shaw's interpretation suggests that Professor Higgins was *the creator* of the image. Now, if we use this characterization to view the role of the principal, we find similarities between Shaw's Professor Higgins and the traditional principal. The traditional change-oriented principal, like Shaw's Henry Higgins, initiates change, is a bold decision maker, and has everything under control; that is, he or she orchestrates all that occurs (in the school). In the original myth, however, Pygmalion did not actually "create" the woman in the marble and "bring her to life." Rather, she existed long before he began to carve. Pygmalion did not bring her into being so much as he delivered her from her marble prison. The differences in interpretation were not lost on Eliza Doolittle nor are they insignificant to school people today.

Grounded in the assumption that people are powerless and unable to control their own destiny, Professor Higgins-like school principals are popularly viewed as people who *make things happen*. Yet this role does not always yield meaningful change in schools. As Fullan (1991) notes:

Grappling with educational change in self-defeating ways has been the modal experience over the last 30 years. . . . The response of many has been to redouble their efforts. For those in authority this has meant more advocacy, more legislation, more accountability, more resources, etc. For those on the receiving end the response has been more closed doors, retreats into isolationism or out of education altogether, and in some cases, collective resistance. We have seen that these seemingly rational political solutions, while perfectly understandable if one is in a hurry to bring about or avoid change, simply do not work. In fact, they do more harm than good as frustration, tension, and despair accumulate. (pp. 345-346)

The NASSP (1996) observes that in schools that achieve successful reform, the principal is not the only school leader; rather, teachers, students, parents, and community members all hold school leadership roles. Wheatley (1992) envisions leaders whose task is to shape their organizations, rather than control them:

What leaders are called upon to do in a chaotic world is to shape their organizations through concepts, not through elaborate rules or structures. (p. 133)

Research has led to an understanding (Fullan, 1996; Hord, 1992; Leithwood, 1992; Leithwood, Tomlinson, & Genge, 1996; Mitchell & Tucker, 1992; Sergiovanni, 1992; Wood, 1998) that principals and others interested in systemic change need to adopt a new style of leadership—facilitative or transformational leadership. This style of leadership encourages participation and replaces leading by control with leading through support. In Conley's (1997) words, "Facilitative notions of leadership require a 'letting go' of the illusion of control and an increasing belief that others can and will function independently and successfully within a common framework of expectations and accountability" (p. 358).

Sergiovanni (1992) describes the advantages of this new leadership style over more traditional leadership models:

[I]nstead of worrying constantly about setting the direction and then engaging teachers and others in a successful march (often known as planning, organizing, leading, motivating, and controlling), the "leader" can focus more on removing obstacles, providing material and emotional support, taking care of the management details that make any journey easier, sharing in the comradeship of the march and in the celebration when the journey is completed, and identifying a new, worthwhile destination for the next march. (pp. 43-44)

Others (Conley, 1997; Fullan, 1996; Hord, 1992; Leithwood, 1992; Mitchell & Tucker, 1992) report that principals who employ facilitative leadership work *interdependently* with teachers, parents, and community members; develop leadership abilities; and encourage active participation in reshaping the school.

Glickman (1991) neatly sums up these views of leadership with his definition of the ideal leadership role for a principal in a school seeking systemic change: "The principal should strive to not be an instructional leader, but rather a leader of instructional leaders" (p. 7).

Professional Development Opportunities

Improving results for students depends upon improving teaching-learning strategies and students' experiences in classrooms. This requires that we improve teachers' professional development, their work orientations, practices and working conditions. (Lawson & Briar-Lawson, 1997, p. 15)

The ubiquitous, one-shot inservice workshops have proven to achieve neither effective changes in teaching practices nor improvements in student learning. Inservice workshops tend to focus on transmitting information and remediating actual classroom practices. Recently, there has been a call (Conley, 1997; Darling-Hammond & Goodwin, 1993; Fullan, 1991; LeCompte & Dworkin, 1991; Lewis, 1997; Slavin, 1989; Sparks & Hirsh, 1997) for a different approach to professional development.

Professional development should be based on the following:

1. Continuous and ongoing critical examination of one's own practices

2. The sharing of ideas with others

3. Learning collaboratively

4. The use of new strategies to promote one's own learning and the learning of others (e.g., building learning communities or communities of learners)[3]

To improve schools, the success of staff development is measured by how it alters instructional behavior; improved performance by students, staff, and the organization; as well as exemplifies that learners create their own knowledge structures rather than merely receive them, according to Sparks and Hirsh (1997). In addition, they stress that staff development must be an integral part of a systems perspective and the systemic change efforts. The most critical is the match between learning and staff development. In their book *A New Vision for Staff Development*, they explain the staff development shift to

1. Individual development and organization development
2. A clear, coherent strategic plan
3. School-focused approaches
4. Focus on student needs and learning outcomes
5. Multiple forms of job-embedded learning
6. Study by teachers of the teaching and learning processes
7. Combination of generic and content-specific skills
8. Staff developers providing consultation, planning, and facilitation as well as training
9. A critical function and major responsibility of all administrators and teacher leaders
10. Continuous improvement for everyone who affects students' learning
11. An indispensable process for reform

Staff development can no longer be something viewed as frivolous. It is a powerful way to form learning communities.

According to Slavin (1989), "The emphasis in staff development must shift from scattershot presentations on what's new to systematic implementation of what works" (p. 757). Professional development is crucial in any attempt to turn a school around. No matter what structure is designed, what rules are enacted, or what curriculum is adopted, if teachers and principals do not acquire the necessary knowledge, skills, and mind-sets, the changes proposed will not be successfully implemented. Researchers now agree that meeting the learning needs of teachers is critical to successful school transformation. They recognize that teachers' learning needs must be met before teachers can meet the needs of students (Cawelti, 1997; Lawson & Briar-Lawson, 1997; Lewis, 1997; NASSP, 1996; Sparks & Hirsh, 1997).

Support

Support is crucial in addressing the difficulties inherent in a troubled school (Hord, 1992; LeCompte & Dworkin, 1991; NASSP, 1996). Teachers and staff members often feel isolated from others, and inservice sessions rarely address specific needs and concerns.

Wood (1995) identifies categories of human and material support that facilitate lasting change for teachers:

Human supports
> Someone who provides recognition and reinforcement
> Someone with whom the teacher can share insights and problems
> Someone to learn from and with

Material supports
> Funds to purchase the services of substitutes to give teachers time for planning, developing, and practicing new skills
> Funds for working one-on-one with other teachers
> Funds to pay for visits to other sites and to pay travel, registration fees, or both, for workshops and conferences

Wood stresses that peers who view themselves as learners and facilitators often provide better support than people who consider themselves experts. To illustrate this point, she relates one teacher's description of the help she received from another teacher in implementing ideas received at a summer institute:

> When I came out of the Institute, I was really fired up; and I kept thinking, "Oh, I'm gonna do this, and I'm gonna do that!" And then when I got in my own classroom, it was scary. I

thought we were gonna have a lot of support from the Institute people, but nobody has been around to help. I didn't know how to actually get started. I probably never would have if Teacher P hadn't been at our school. I had gone in and talked to her on several occasions and told her "I'd really like to do this, but I'm having a hard time getting started." . . . She said, "Okay, I'll come in and demonstrate a lesson." . . . All I needed was some direction. . . . Even after she had given me some ideas, I still needed to go to her and say, "Well, what do they mean by this? What exactly do I need to do here?" I just needed her there to know that I was doing okay. (p. 42)

Fellow faculty members can provide much needed nurturing and assistance; however, administrators, such as the principal, curriculum specialists, and central office personnel, must also provide support if a school is truly to turn itself around.

Site-Based Management

Designed to transform roles and responsibilities, site-based management calls for teachers, students, parents, and community representatives to become involved in school decision-making enterprises.

Site-based management comes up in virtually all discussions of school restructuring. Researchers credit effective site-based management with higher decision quality; increased satisfaction, commitment, and morale; and reduced resistance to change (Arterbury & Hord, 1991; Hallinger & Richardson, 1988; Keith, 1996; E. Miller, 1995; Newmann, 1993; Wood, 1984, 1989).

In the 1980s, researchers assumed site-based management would create improved teaching and learning environments as well as enhance student performance. More recent literature suggests that site-based management facilitates school and student improvement only when individuals participate in decision making that specifically addresses teaching and learning issues (Arterbury & Hord, 1991;

Cawelti, 1997; Fullan, 1993b; Keith, 1996; Miller, 1995). Conley (1997) notes:

> Changes in governance may be critical to restructuring when they occur along with other activities designed to enhance student learning and when they function to support this goal. Changes in governance appear to hold the greatest promise as a means to ends, not ends in themselves. (p. 329)

It is becoming clear that involving parents and other community members in decisions made regarding the school and students is important (Cawelti, 1997; Conley, 1997; Lawson & Briar-Lawson, 1997; NASSP, 1996). School leaders must rethink ways to involve their communities. Inviting the community to the school to be entertained or to assist in PTA fund-raising functions is not sufficient to bring about substantive change. Community members must have opportunities to participate in the educational process, to assist students in their work, and to engage in decision-making ventures regarding students' future learning.

Berliner (1997) underlines the importance of involving parents and community members in school-related activities and of seeking their assistance regarding school matters:

> [S]chool administrators have given too much time to the internal forces in their buildings and districts, and too little attention to the external forces that have an impact on them. I think if you do the same math I do you will see why this is a problem. Take the waking hours of a typical child between birth and 17 years of age (16 hours per day × 365 days per year × 17 years = 99,280 hours). Ask how many of those are school hours (6 hours per day × 180 days per year × 12 years of schooling = 12,960)? The percent of waking hours spent in neighborhoods and with family is 87 percent. The amount of time spent in school is 13 percent. Which socializing agency has the better chance to influence the child's attitudes, values, habits and goals? Clearly the family and community are the primary influences on a child. (p. 14)

Summary

The lessons learned from *How to Turn a School Around* can be attributed to each of the factors discussed and presented in the overviews of literature presented in this chapter. A faculty has to work together to map out the route toward reform. As the faculty learns together through professional development and makes decisions together, they seek out support for their efforts.

Chapter 2 calls attention to the importance of designating the mission, vision, and goals of the reform effort. The chapter provides examples of strategies used by schools for school reform efforts that are consistent with current reform literature.

Notes

1. Conley (1997) makes a useful distinction between: (a) renewal activities, (b) reform-driven activities, and (c) restructuring activities. He describes *renewal activities* as those that assist the school to do a better, more efficient job of doing what it already is doing. *Reform-driven activities* actually "alter existing procedures, rules and requirements to enable the organization to adapt the way it functions to new circumstances or requirements" that have been initiated by external forces such as the board of education or the state legislature. While renewal and reform-driven activities may produce new rules and procedures, *restructuring activities* focus on changing "fundamental assumptions, practices, and relationships, both within the organization and between the organization and the outside world, in ways that lead to improved and varied student-learning outcomes" (p. 9).

2. In large part, the two opening paragraphs of this section are adapted from Wood (1995, pp. 67-68).

3. A community of learners has been differentiated from a learning community by Wood (1998): "the phrase *community of learners* is used to describe a collection of individuals who are desirous of continuous learning and who pursue opportunities to improve their knowledge and skills so that their instructional capabilities will improve. The phrase . . . *learning community* [is] used to signal that people, in the context of a group, are collaborating in a number of ways: learning together, building on each other's strengths, sharing, and helping each other to become what they are capable of becoming" (p. 1103).

Setting Direction

Chapter Focus

The focus of this chapter is setting direction. The chapter's first section highlights literature about vision and mission. Later sections look at experiences relating to adopting a vision, articulating a mission, and ultimately developing an action plan. This combination—vision, mission, action plan—sets the direction for faculty reform.

Key Insights From the Literature About Vision and Mission

A school's vision and mission provide a sense of purpose and can motivate participation in the effort, according to Milstein (1993). In order to make strides toward excellence, a school's staff and community have to reach agreement on roles and make purposes clear. An examination of trends, future forecasting, and priorities is necessary in order to develop a relevant mission.

Discussion of purposes and trends requires facilitation. Facilitative leadership is a key factor in the process of change, according to research-based evidence. Facilitative leadership provides guidance and support for school change that meets the needs of all children, particularly those at risk. According to Hord (1992), developing a vision focused on improved effectiveness is central to facilitative leadership. Vision is one's preferred image of the future. Facilitative leadership articulates a vision that is, hopefully, developed jointly by a school's faculty and administration. On occasion, however, leaders influence others to accept a vision to which they did not initially contribute. Either way, they need to come to view it as their own.

A vision may not necessarily be fully achieved. It is an idealistic dream, an intangible aspiration. However, Cunningham and Gresso (1993) argue that visions provide direction, a sense of pride, and are worth aspiring to over time. They view development of a vision as the first step in an educational organization's move toward high performance. A shared vision can eventually tie the culture of the organization together. Consistent attention focused on vision by leaders can inspire action toward achieving it. In turn, with a common vision, members of the organization can be motivated to higher levels of performance.

Even though visions are deemed necessary for success in educational reform (Fullan, 1993a), visions come with action. In other words, within the educational organization, there is work being done to create change and improvement. As this work is pursued, a vision begins to take form. The school community has the opportunity to develop ownership for the vision; to think about the actions taken, their meanings; and to understand the primary purposes of their school. Leaders can make clear what they support, what they promote and hope to accomplish for the school. Faculty and community observe whether the words spoken by leaders are put into practice. As actions are undertaken together by the school and community, a vision takes shape.

Change efforts and improvements are usually initiated before a vision is fully developed. However, as a clear and shared vision is formed, it can contribute a stronger sense of direction to planning and coordinating programs and designing instructional strategies (Peterson, 1995). A shared vision can also maintain the focus on student learning.

To be truly shared, a vision should be developed through a process that involves input from members of the school and its community and should articulate their hopes, dreams, values, and ideals for the school. To guide direction effectively and consistently, the vision should also be stated clearly, displayed prominently, and communicated frequently (Peterson, 1996).

Tewel (1993) asserts that the first step in creating the capacity for change is to recognize that some things are in need of improvement. He suggests a whole-school reform approach in which long-term vision transforms both the process of work and its outcomes. Whole-school reform in schools departs dramatically from approaches based on crisis management and limited projects (Barth, 1990; Schlechty, 1990; Tewel, 1993). Staff in schools undergoing whole-school reform develop a strong staff-wide commitment to both short- and long-term school goals. Like Sizer and Hord, Tewel stresses the importance of collective vision in working toward school reform.

Vision is an ideal that energizes a school staff toward meaningful and valued action, according to Starratt (1995). Leaders facilitate the articulation of the vision in such a way that generates enthusiasm among the school's members by being sure that the vision includes their dreams and aspirations. A vision that embraces members' collective beliefs can lead to shared agreements and celebrations. If the vision is entwined in policies, programs, and procedures, it can further energize daily efforts.

A school's mission is often expressed as a mission statement, which should be a succinct expression of the purpose of the school stated with intended outcomes. It should proclaim what the school stands for and what it hopes to accomplish. A carefully crafted mission statement can serve as a guide for decision making and resource allocation (Milstein, 1993). A school's mission statement should support a district mission and be the anchor for goal setting and action planning.

Goals are broad statements that will lead toward the mission. A school's mission statement has to be more than mere words. Everyone involved with the school must take the necessary steps to make the mission reality. Those steps are expressed as goals that are fundamental ideals or statements of where the organization wants to be. Goal setting is a process to formulate how to proceed or to map out the journey to achieve the mission. Goals should be written to be clearly understood; challenging, yet possible; motivating to those asked to participate; and measurable as to the extent they are achieved (Milstein, 1993).

However, it should not be expected that the mapped journey will be easy. A goal-oriented journey that requires change typically produces uncertainty, anxiety, and difficulties, as well as learning (Fullan, 1993a). Individuals have to be risk takers and the school climate needs to be one that encourages risk taking. For others to gain a sense of ownership of the process and of the goals is a frustrating, time-consuming course, according to Sarason (1996). It takes time and energy for a faculty and community to be directly involved in determining the direction through goals for the change process.

Another way to view goal setting is as an empowering covenant, the term used by Starratt (1995) to emphasize that it is an operative and express agreement entered into by members of a community. An empowering covenant guides the activities and decisions. Goal setting should be an empowering covenant because it is based on deeply held values and commitments. Goal setting will thus utilize everyone's talents to work together as a group with a focus and intensity on the goals and mission.

An action plan should include short-range and long-range goals that address the mission of the school. The plan identifies who will do what, when, and how, in order to achieve changes in the school. The plan should be written with evaluative measurement standards and provide specific direction for actions to be taken by the staff and community. An action plan that is developed with widespread involvement of stakeholders increases the chances that it will be clear, agreed on, and followed with commitment (Milstein, 1993).

A Visioning Approach

An example of a visioning approach is the Coalition of Essential Schools (CES). The philosophy and tenets of the CES, a national school reform movement, has profoundly influenced reform efforts. Founded in 1984 by Theodore Sizer, CES responds to Sizer's (1984) critique of American education, *Horace's Compromise*. The Nine Common Principles of the Coalition of Essential Schools provide a philosophical framework for school reform through improved teaching and learning rather than through application of a specific reform model (see Appendix). Sizer's focus is on the point where teacher, student, and subject matter come together. He strongly advocates idea sharing among Coalition members, and stresses that school members must shape their own schools, always with respect for the communities of which they are a part.

Sizer (1992) published findings from his reform work with approximately 200 schools in 23 states over a 7-year period. In summarizing these findings, Sizer made the following observations:

1. Each school's plan uniquely actualizes the Nine Common Principles of the Coalition of Essential Schools.
2. Leadership and support are important.
3. Conflict arises over desire for status quo, change, and the refusal to take sides.
4. Helpers—critical friends from outside the school—can assist school reform.
5. Incentives can boost the process of change.

Sizer published his research to assist schools embarked on reform. By offering insights about reform, Sizer hoped to enable school members to overcome challenges and minimize pitfalls that often characterize the road to reform. Ultimately, as promoted through CES and as offered by Sizer, CES's principles provide a framework for school vision and mission building. School faculties are using the framework and the approach offered by the CES to establish or refine their reform process.

The Faculty's Role in Establishing a Vision

Faculty and staff may adopt, modify, or develop their own vision. For example, some schools begin with the adoption and modification of CES's Nine Principles. Faculty members define the meaning of the Nine Principles in their own words and develop their own purposes of schooling. In the process, they begin to refocus the purpose of their work, but more tasks lie ahead. To make a vision work, the faculty has to internalize it, make the vision its own. As well as articulating a cohesive vision, the faculty needs to agree on a realistic, achievable mission. Finally, it has to map out an action plan based on intended goals.

An example of using these processes can be found at Kennedy High School. Developing the school's interpretation of CES's Nine Principles during an inservice day became the faculty's first step toward establishing a vision and mission. Adopting the Nine Principles was the starting point for Kennedy's faculty to begin to refocus its purpose. Constant reminders of and discussion about the Principles guided the faculty through the reform process. The faculty undertook professional development, through which it articulated a mission, conducted needs assessments, and developed an action plan for defining and achieving specific goals. Within a year, the school's culture began to change. Trust was built among the faculty, and they started to focus on systemic work toward school improvement. The revised Principles were then posted in each classroom.

The Faculty's Role in Establishing a Mission

There will be differences in how faculty members view their role in school reform, school mission, and student education. Open discussion about opinions and perceptions is integral to reaching agreement in these areas (Muncey & McQuillan, 1993). As faculty members at a school express themselves regarding their beliefs and aspirations for the school, the communication helps them establish a clearer, more collective vision.

To develop the school's mission, time must be set aside for faculty members to concentrate on the "whys" of their work:

- Why have they chosen to teach?
- Why should they attempt to change the school?
- Why are they at the particular school?
- What is unique about their school?

Participation by the entire faculty can give everyone an opportunity to have input into the mission statement. In addition to looking at the "whys" of their work, faculty members may also want to explore their expectations of professional development and write about the philosophies and platforms informing their individual educational outlooks.

After such an effort, Kennedy High School faculty responses included, among others, "To see our school improve for faculty and students . . ." In expressing the expectation of the professional development sessions, one person stated, "To learn what this [reform approach] is and how to implement it." Some members anticipated that further sessions would teach them skills that they would then practice in the classroom. These responses and others revealed some misunderstanding among faculty members. Instead of comprehending a process-oriented approach to reform, they thought the workshops were to be focused on a curriculum or skill to be incorporated into their teaching. Only one response expressed a negative expectation: "I expect these sessions to be a lot of work, and I really don't expect them to accomplish a whole lot. It's just more work for teachers!"

At another inservice session, faculty members worked in teams to draw pictures of their ideal school. This required faculty members to develop further their beliefs about education and to link them to the school's physical environment. Teams were instructed to use various colored markers, plain flip chart paper, and not to use written words to draw their ideal school. The teams were then asked to explain their drawings to each other; they took great pride in their drawing's physical representations of their beliefs. As constant reminders of their visions of better schools for students and teachers, the drawings were then displayed in the school.

Developing a school's interpretation of a mission takes time and effort. Once the faculty agrees on a mission statement, publicizing it and communicating it becomes the next step toward establishing a direction. With the mission statement posted in each classroom, the teachers can refer to it as they proceed through the year. The school's mission statement can also be prominently displayed in the main entrance and in the office.

Goal Setting

The discussions about a vision, mission, and the purposes of a school help to articulate goals of the school. Goal setting is a process involving educators and community whereby they can jointly identify the purpose of the school and what can be expected from the school. They can also identify what students will accomplish by the time they exit or graduate from the school. Fleshing out a vision builds shared purposes and beliefs that can produce a powerful bond around common themes that emphasize what is important and what is valued (Sergiovanni, 1991). The goals, decisions, and ongoing activities should be congruent with the vision and mission of the school.

In one school, goals were initially drafted by the school improvement team composed of teachers and parents. While they were involved in drafting the goals, their work was supported by a district mission statement and district goals as well as a school mission statement. Those mission statements and the district goals served as a framework or guidelines for the school goals. In other words, the team attempted to come up with goals that were specific to their community yet in line with the district goals. The school goals were reviewed by the entire faculty for further input from teachers. Then, the team shared the goals with the larger community in a community forum for further input and revision of the goals. When the goals were shared verbally and in written form, explanations were provided and opportunities for questions and concerns. In one instance, the teachers quickly received the message that the community was not supportive of early released time for teachers because of the hardship on parents for child care. The teachers listened to the concerns and found another way to increase faculty planning time without disrupting the community's routines. The goals became the focus for the school's action plan. Each year, the goals and action plan are reviewed for progress and adjustments.

Developing an Action Plan

One of the first steps to developing an action plan is to have the faculty study or become familiar with school reform, the use of data for assessment and evaluation purposes, decision-making strategies, team-building skills, and the steps involved in action planning. The faculty can discuss school reform and improvement processes and become acquainted with various models for reform. They can also learn how to gather data and incorporate it into decision making.

For starters, a faculty should focus on school assessment for action planning. Conducting a needs assessment can provide baseline data to measure and document change and to reveal focus areas for action planning. During the needs assessment process, faculty and community may want to use the areas identified in the effective schools research, such as

- A. Leadership
- B. High Expectations
- C. Instructional Focus
- D. School Climate
- E. Community Relations
- F. Monitoring

Or, faculty members may discuss the school's status in areas such as:

- A. Communication (horizontal and vertical)
- B. Teaching Strategies/Student Performance
- C. School and Community Partnerships (including school-to-work)
- D. Evaluation Strategies

At Kennedy, the faculty divided into groups, each of which explored one of these areas. Each group broke its area into subcategories and assessed Kennedy's status in each subcategory. The groups then reported their conclusions back to the faculty at large. After some discussion, the faculty, working in small groups, began drafting action plans to address areas of perceived weakness. Once the information was gathered and compiled, it was distributed to all. At a follow-up session, faculty members reviewed recommendations and voted on areas to target for reform in their final action plan. In this manner, the faculty as a whole determined which needs were the most pressing and would therefore receive focused attention. At a subsequent session, a consultant facilitated the formulation of the school's action plan.

Assessing and developing action plans can bring everyone's thoughts and opinions into the open. Staff members can be given copies of the plan and be encouraged to hold each other accountable for participation in the actions that are identified.

A faculty's action plan is basically a school improvement plan. Each school year, the faculty should use the plan as a basis to discuss progress toward goals, focus on strengths and weaknesses, and update its plan to reflect changing needs. The plan can continue to provide direction for the faculty and becomes an administrative tool by the forwarding of school progress reports to the district office. The faculty can use its annual plan review and update activity to give new staff a better sense of the school's goals and accomplishments. With continuous updating, review, evaluation, and revision, a school's plan can provide direction for its faculty and for school growth overall.

Summary

Time has to be set aside for faculty members to discuss their views of the school's future and their beliefs of the purpose of schooling. Leaders can facilitate the process and encourage everyone's participation. By working together, a vision and mission can be agreed on. Goals directed toward fulfilling the mission can be developed. Then, an action plan geared toward the mission and goals can be jointly developed. The continuous cycle of agreeing on, implementing, monitoring, and evaluating an educational improvement plan keeps a faculty focused on goals and a plan of action. By evaluating progress annually, needed modifications can keep purposes on track, and new staff members can be engaged in the effort to serve the school's mission.

Professional Development

Chapter Focus

Chapter 3 focuses on the relationship between professional development and school reform. Chapter sections review key findings about professional development and offer educators professional development ideas that may be applied to reforming schools. The chapter explores how professional development may be implemented, funded, achieved, and delivered.

Key Insights From the Literature About Professional Development

In *Sculpting the Learning Organization*, Watkins and Marsick (1993) define a learning organization as "one that learns continuously and transforms itself. Learning takes place in individuals, teams, the organization, and even the communities in which the organization interacts" (p. 8). Watkins and Marsick identify an institution's ability to act as a learning organization as vital to its ability to respond to the changing nature of work, changes in the workforce, and changes in how people learn. By their nature, learning organizations seek transformational change, which is key to expanding organizational capacity. Therefore, one desirable outcome of school reform is for a school to become a learning organization. One way of thinking of becoming a learning organization is through professional development.

Most leaders in school reform identify professional development as a key factor in achieving school success. For example, one obstacle to reform reported by SERVE (SouthEastern Regional Vision for Education, 1994) in its study of barriers to effective reform is underinvestment in training and professional development. A close examination of state spending patterns reveals that training and professional development have not been seen as school reform priorities. For example, it has been recommended by the American Society for Training and Development that effective organizations earmark about 3% of payroll and fringe benefits for staff training and development. Yet, the study found that less than one third of 1% of state-funded payroll and fringe benefits are set aside for training its educators. To compound the problem, time for teachers to meet for quality planning or training is not extensive, so teachers receive little training on the job. SERVE's study found that both lack of planning time and lack of training hamper reform.

Professional development is crucial to schools engaged in systemic change. It can help the faculty not only understand change processes, but to support change. Teacher learning thus becomes an approach for supplementing change and for motivating staff toward continuous school improvement (Arnold, 1995). In Arnold's view, professional development

- Generates support for change
- Provides understanding of change processes
- Assists faculty in implementing change
- Motivates staff toward sustained change

To vitalize change from within, Arnold proposes scheduling time for professional development during the teacher workday.

Fullan (1991) notes that bad professional development experiences have given professional development a negative image. He suggests that school districts and schools avoid such experiences by recognizing the extra energy change requires and by initiating and supporting continuous staff development as a means of distributing that energy across time. According to Fullan (1991), in order to produce positive results, staff development must incorporate the National Staff Development Council's (NSDC) "Characteristics of Effective Staff Development Activities." Five of these characteristics were incorporated in the case settings used in this book:

1. *Involvement in planning*
   Staff development activities tend to be more effective when participants have taken part in identifying objectives and planning activities.

2. *Time for planning*
   Whether staff development activities are mandatory or voluntary, participants need time away from their regular teaching or administrative responsibilities in order to plan for program changes.

3. *Involvement of principals*
   Staff development activities in which principals are active participants are more effective. Active involvement means that principals need to participate in activities in which their teachers are involved.

4. *District administrative support*
   For staff development activities to be effective, district-level support (e.g., human and financial resources) needs to be active and visible.

5. *Expectations*
   Participants should know what is expected of them during the activities, as well as what they will be asked to do when the experience is over.

Professional development efforts need conscientiously and consistently to embody the NSDC characteristics. It is understood that some characteristics present greater challenges to incorporation. In cases where professional development seems in danger of not possessing one or more NSDC characteristics, intervention strategies can be employed.

First, principals can foster a sense of participation and belonging. For example, one of the challenges facing a principal in relation to professional development is determining who will receive it. Schools often make professional development available to only a select few. Not surprisingly, these few participants are labeled favorites, and the faculties at these schools become divided. An ethnographic study of eight charter CES schools conducted between 1986 and 1990 found that "a core of faculty members became active in their school's reform, but their efforts often ended up dividing the faculty" (Muncey & McQuillan, 1993, p. 488). If only a core group of faculty members receive professional development, it can result in divisiveness and accusations of favoritism.

Professional development activities offered to the entire faculty can be used to foster faculty participation and open communication. School administrators further demonstrate their support for professional development by setting aside time during faculty meetings and giving faculty members released time during the school day. Workshops regarding school reform, change processes, and team building can further the process of reform because of common understanding.

Second, as Fullan (1991) notes, staff development is related to change in practice. He explains that staff development must be ongoing, interactive, and provide cumulative learning to develop new concepts, skills, and behaviors.

Third, according to Tewel (1991), principals wanting to create an atmosphere responsive to change need to provide teachers with the opportunity to plan together and to work collaboratively in order to solve problems and develop new initiatives. Communication is vital when a school wants to pursue change. The entire faculty must be a part of the change process, especially in school analysis, action planning, and setting the direction of the school.

Finding the Resources to Provide Professional Development

Professional development often has a low budgetary priority in school districts, so providing professional development presents a real challenge to principals.

Even with the practice of making allocations to school sites, school districts simply do not allocate sufficient monies to professional development activities. Because professional development can be a positive driving force in school reform, it cannot be ignored. Administrators who perceive the importance of professional development can overcome many obstacles, obtain resources, and be sure that it is provided in meaningful ways. By successfully employing a variety of approaches to accessing funds for professional development, demonstrating commitment to the necessity of professional development, and identifying creative ways of finding the required time, principals can play an important leadership role. Following are some strategies used by schools to integrate professional development into their educational missions.

The likelihood of obtaining resources is higher when applicants have established relationships with individuals within organizations that support reform. Firsthand knowledge of the organization's interests, goals, and time frames is also helpful, particularly in determining whether congruence exists between what the funding organization supports and what the school seeks to achieve. It is also worth noting that receiving support from one organization often increases other organizations' willingness to offer support.

Outside funding also can help teachers and staff make the most of the professional development opportunities it creates. At Kennedy High School, staff recognized that the school district and the outside organizations that funded their professional development would follow progress closely. This recognition motivated the faculty to take professional development seriously in order to demonstrate its positive effects and the district's and outside organizations' wisdom in investing in Kennedy High.

Kennedy High School received its first professional development grant through state funding linked to the Coalition of Essential Schools. The $5,000 grant provided targeted funding for school visits, professional conferences, consultants, substitutes, and extended contracts for summer curriculum development.

Seek Funds/Grants for Professional Development

Funds to support professional development need to be set aside in the school district's budget. Whether centralized or decentralized, each school district typically has its own procedure for requesting additional funds. Some school districts require written proposals to secure funds, others stipulate discussion with the superintendent. Even if a district is not currently allocating funds for site-specific professional development, initiating requests for such funds can be an effective means for bringing the district's attention to a need that may have been overlooked.

School administrators also can channel internal funds to support professional development efforts. The superintendent for Kennedy High School's district responded to the principal's initial request for professional development funds by telling him that before the district would allocate funds, the principal would first have to demonstrate that he could improve discipline and maintain order. It was important for students to be self-disciplined before substitutes could go into the classrooms to release teachers for professional development. Once the school had been stabilized, the superintendent authorized expenditures for substitute teacher costs and for tuition and fees relating to professional development courses and activities. With increased substitute teacher funding, faculty members were able to obtain released time to participate in workshops, make school visitations, and attend professional conferences. In all, the district allocated approximately $10,000 to Kennedy High School for professional development.

There also are external funding sources. Many federal, state, and private organizations have recognized that if school improvement is to take place, professional development must be pursued. These organizations often have funds, in the form of grants, that they will award to schools or districts for professional development. Soliciting special grants from these and other organizations does not require professional grant-writing skills. Often the providers themselves will offer assistance to write and complete grant applications.

Create Time for Professional Development

The value of teaching time for students is indisputable, but the value to teachers of time taken during the school day to enhance their professional learning must also be recognized and made a priority. Administrators need to create time to plan and implement professional development and then give such initiatives their full support.

As Chapter 2 outlined, facilitative leadership for change is necessary both to increasing student success and to guide and support effective school change (Hord, 1992). In studies of school change, training is one of four functional classifications of interventions most frequently used by facilitative leaders. Finding the time to provide such training is one of facilitative leadership's greatest challenges. A few strategies that might be considered include:

Before- and After-School Meetings. When time during the day simply cannot be made available, professional development sessions can be held before or after school. Although not ideal, before- and after-school sessions are steps in the right direction, and certainly are preferable to not offering professional development activities. Before- and after-school faculty professional development sessions can serve to increase motivation about the change process and can demonstrate to possible funding sources the value of released time for effecting reform. If such sessions improve school success, district administrators will likely be encouraged to provide support and funds for released time as an investment in successful school change.

At one school, professional development took the form of a series of biweekly after-school faculty sessions focused on school improvement. Finding the most convenient day of the week for all staff to attend the 30- to 45-minute meetings presented a challenge. Teachers agreed to brief each other in the event that meeting times conflicted with other school or outside commitments. Attendance at these sessions was high because faculty members knew they would be involved in decisions about their school.

Combination of Before-/After-School Meetings and Released Time. Offering professional development during the teachers' work hours declares a school's commitment to reform. In order to provide released time, substitutes may have to be obtained, or the district may have to build in workdays identified for professional development. A compromise is a combination of released time and before- or after-school meetings for professional development sessions. Such a combination can provide ongoing professional development at the school site for reform purposes. These sessions can be held throughout the school year to enhance continuity.

Kennedy High School carried out formal professional development activities comprised of a sequence of before- and after-school and released time workshops. Because the workshops and activities explored topics such as school reform, change processes, and team building, a local university approved the sequence for continuing education credit. The district's Assistant Superintendent was designated as course instructor, and the district agreed to pay half the cost of tuition for faculty members interested in taking the course for college credit. The salary schedule rewards additional training and experience, so teachers who received credit also received salary increases.

Kennedy High School's approach provided field-based instruction responsive to site-specific needs. At the same time, it established an alliance among the school, the school district, and a local university.

Engage Administrators as Substitutes. Sometimes there are no funds to secure substitutes to provide teachers with released time for professional development. Similarly, a union contract may not permit school administrators to require teachers to devote time before or after school for professional development. In such cases, a school leader has to seek alternative ways of providing time for teachers to be engaged in professional development. For example, the principal of one school convinced central office administrators to serve as substitute teachers an hour at a time in classrooms. This approach extended professional development opportunities to everyone. It enabled teachers to participate in planning sessions for school improvement on a rotating basis and gave central office administrators a chance to gain firsthand knowledge of the challenges facing teachers in the classroom.

Providing professional development must be a creative endeavor. In addition to the approaches listed here, administrators, faculty, and staff can also explore approaches uniquely suited to their own school's situation, including approaches that may not require additional costs. Indeed, as proposed next, the most effective professional development programs are often those that arise from a combination of different approaches and deliver a variety of professional developmental opportunities.

Delivering Professional Development

Thus far, the chapter has described *how* schools can pursue professional development, how sources for funding might be found and secured, and how time for professional development delivery might be created. The rest of the chapter explores the *whats* of professional development: characteristics that make professional development effective, methods for delivering professional development that provide the overall best assurances of staff learning and school improvement, and, finally, examples of what some schools are doing to incorporate these characteristics and methods into their own professional development programs.

Because professional development plays such a key role in school reform, researchers recognize that it works best when delivered in a variety of ways, and works worst when it is offered, as sometimes occurs, as a "one-shot" or "fix-it" approach to school difficulties (Tewel, 1991). Sparks and Loucks-Horsley (1989) define five staff development models (SDM):

1. Individually guided staff development, focusing on personal plans for professional learning
2. Observation-assessment focusing on analysis of teaching practices
3. Involvement and opportunities for teachers to participate in developmental and improvement processes
4. Training workshops and other activities to learn new skills and acquire new knowledge
5. Inquiry-problem-solving for teachers emphasizing data collection and data analysis

Each of these models can benefit faculty; however, the best and most successful professional development opportunities that also promote school improvement are those that provide an appropriate combination of aspects of all five types.

Professional development at schools studied by the authors of this book demonstrated the recommendations of Sparks and

Loucks-Horsley (1989) by (a) following a variety of approaches and (b) using a combination of staff development models within each approach and across the program as a whole. Those schools' approaches fall into six categories:

1. On-site workshops/courses
2. Informal professional development
3. Visitations to other schools
4. Attendance at professional conferences
5. Presentations to their faculty by teachers from other schools
6. Presentations by their faculty to teachers at other schools

These categories will be described in practice as they relate to the Sparks and Loucks-Horsley staff development models.

On-Site Workshops/Courses

Workshops and other activities designed for teachers to learn new skills or to acquire new knowledge can be offered at the school site. The importance of the skills and knowledge being presented is emphasized by bringing the activities to the school. To send a clear message that workshop participation is expected of everyone, attendance should be made easily accessible. Prior planning with staff involvement in decision making regarding workshop offerings can increase ownership. Staff involvement in planning also increases the probability that professional development will be relevant to the faculty's needs.

A series of workshops focused on school reform can encourage focus to put time and effort into the process. A series of workshops can even be developed as a university course to offer college credit hours. An important aspect is to offer the activity so that all faculty members can participate, bringing the staff together to interact, discuss, ponder, challenge, and reach some agreements regarding school reform.

Kennedy High School faculty members did not readily embrace professional development when it was first introduced. Indeed, they viewed professional development and any reform activity with great skepticism. None the less, professional development became a driving force in reform activities at Kennedy High School. Faculty at Kennedy attended an on-site university course focused on school reform and received a subsidy from the district for half the tuition cost. The local university school of education head conducted course registration at Kennedy High, and the assistant superintendent acted as course instructor at no expense to the district or the university. The principal actively participated in most course sessions, but discreetly absented himself when the teachers used these sessions as a forum to critique his leadership and his direction of the school.

As part of the coursework, a group of teachers who volunteered to assist with planning joined together to form the Research Committee (RC). After the first two sessions, the principal, assistant superintendent, and members of the RC met to review initial activities and make plans for future sessions and workshops. They reviewed the faculty members' expectation statements and noted their readiness to diagnose the status quo situation at the school. The planning group decided to solicit consultants to guide the school faculty through a faculty-driven school analysis approach focusing on gathering baseline data to measure school needs, documenting change, and establishing focus areas for action planning.

As one faculty member noted of his participation in the on-site professional development activities, self-examination and examination of the school grew naturally from Kennedy High School's professional development activities:

> Some of the good things that have come out from the workshops have been the discussion that has taken place, a realization that, perhaps, faculty is part of the problem. I think in the past . . . we would always talk about the students being the problem, that students can't learn. . . . Maybe, I have to change. Maybe it's me. And I think as faculty, if you approach it on that basis, I think we are going to be more successful.

Kennedy High School's approach to providing on-site activities meets the criteria defined in the Sparks and Loucks-Horsley model of involvement and training. Coursework established faculty participation in activities related to school reform processes and provided training in assessment, data-gathering, analysis, and team-building skills.

Emphasis on professional development for all staff signals a new approach to school change. Its effects can have an immense, positive impact on the faculty's progress with school reform.

Informal Professional Development

Informal professional development can be initiated by individuals or encouraged by school leaders. Informal opportunities for adult learning can contribute to the school becoming a learning organization. It is a natural, relaxed approach to professional development when a teacher or principal offers verbal information or printed material that adds to an individual's professional growth.

As an example, throughout the school year, administrators at Kennedy High distributed articles and other readings about school reform to the faculty, both as part of formal professional development activities and as a supplement to less formal professional development activities. On occasion, faculty members shared readings on their own, seeking information about topics such as specific teaching strategies. Faculty discussion of readings frequently moved beyond the professional development session and continued in departmental meetings, across departments, and in informal settings such as the faculty lounge.

As an informal approach to professional development, faculty reading and discussion embodies the Sparks and Loucks-Horsley model of individually guided staff development. Administrators can be the primary means of delivery, but faculty members can determine content for themselves and make decisions about how to apply the information provided to their own individual situations. Some faculty members may even use readings to develop professional development plans required by the district for performance evaluation.

Visitations to Other Schools

Faculty visitations to other schools allow teachers to see what other educators are doing in their classrooms and how they are responding to the challenges of shaping school change. Through visitations, faculty members often "see themselves in a different setting," a process that gives them new and clearer insights into their own reform work. Faculty members can begin to formulate specific questions in relation to their observations of other school programs: How do faculty members at these schools arrive at their teaching methods? How do they feel about reform? Which aspects of other approaches work? Which do not? Such visitations can help to shape responses to these and other questions and give faculty members valuable information regarding their own classroom and school-wide efforts.

During the first year of engaging Kennedy faculty members in school visitation, one noted that ". . . widening horizons is always a good thing." Another said, "Ideally, I would like to see all teachers go out and visit a couple of different schools because we tend to get very inbred here."

School visitation continued through the second and third years of reform. Faculty visited schools in teams and used the drive back to school to discuss and analyze their observations and to determine how what they learned applied to their own situation. Presentations to the rest of the faculty linked these observations to processes at their own school and addressed both the positive and negative implications of other schools' experiences as they related to their own challenges.

School visitation is closely linked to Sparks and Loucks-Horsley's inquiry model. Faculty members can analyze their observations of other schools and use these analyses to query and measure their own reform efforts. They also can adopt and adapt other schools' approaches. In presenting their conclusions to the rest of the staff, the faculty can demonstrate to the rest of the faculty how they might apply different strategies in their classrooms.

Attendance at Professional Conferences

Professional conferences offer opportunities for teachers and staff to gain knowledge and skills while interacting with colleagues from other schools. It is most beneficial for teachers to attend professional conferences where topics in school reform are being investigated. Attendance can be based on general interest, the curriculum one teaches, or on representing the school at the request of an administrator. There are numerous professional conferences held throughout the nation that offer quality presentations (e.g., Association for Curriculum Development, American Association of School Administrators, National Staff Development Council, and also state/local conferences). Most of these conferences host an array of selections of sessions to attend.

The lessons and insights derived from attending a professional conference can also be shared with those who do not attend. Because only a few faculty members can be freed up and supported to attend a professional conference, they can share information with other teachers at a faculty meeting when they return. Copies of articles or material from the conference can be selected for distribution and subsequent discussion with other faculty members. Often, additional materials can be made available for those interested in obtaining more information about specific topics. Throughout the course of a school year or over a few years, opportunities to attend professional conferences can be rotated so that different individuals get this experience. By spreading out these opportunities, everyone eventually has a chance to participate.

Thanks to funding obtained from outside sources, faculty members at Kennedy High School were able to attend such national conferences as the Coalition of Essential Schools and the National Restructuring Institute, where they gathered information and materials about reform development and implementation. During the first year in which funds were available, faculty teams attended a national conference focused on restructuring secondary schools and a research seminar focused on an interdisciplinary approach to strengthening English and social studies. The following year, a faculty group attended a regional institute of the Coalition of Essential Schools.

Attendance at professional conferences is an illustration of development through involvement and training. Faculty members who attend conferences can gain new skills and knowledge and share them with their fellow colleagues through work groups, presentations, and informal discussion. As a result, all faculty members are able to participate in applying the knowledge and skills gained by individual faculty members who attend conferences toward school improvement because the information obtained can be used in school improvement processes.

Conference attendance also supports Sparks and Loucks-Horsley's concept of individually guided staff development. The experience of being an attendee—conferring with peers from other communities, staying in quality environments, and reporting their activities to fellow staff—can help faculty members validate a sense of themselves as professionals engaged in professional activities.

Presentations by Teachers From Other Schools

Visiting other schools influences identification of teachers who can be invited to make presentations at the school engaged in reform efforts. Attendance at professional conferences can also help identify educators to invite. When a school is involved in reform, there is a need to learn from others. This can be facilitated by seeking out the experiences of other schools. Sometimes these contacts can come through referral by consultants, state department officials, or administrators. School leaders can make initial contacts to gain some basic information before invitations are offered, but it may be appropriate to have a teacher speak directly to someone from other schools rather than have an administrator act as an intermediate.

When faculty were exploring various models for class scheduling at Kennedy High, they invited teachers who had developed alternative approaches at other schools to discuss their scheduling experiences. The guest teachers addressed some of the difficulties generated by new class scheduling, instructional approaches, and ideas for making changes in the classroom.

Presentations by Faculty at Other Schools

Not only can teachers be involved in their own development and improvement process, but through making presentations they also learn as well as share by becoming involved in those processes with faculty members at other schools. Preparing for and making presentations help teachers clarify reform dynamics as well as share enthusiasm and pride in the faculty's achievements.

A principal can also keep funding agencies and other schools informed of the teachers' accomplishments and the progress of reform

at the school. Concerted efforts to acknowledge the faculty's achievements whenever possible can be an important intrinsic reward as well
as provide support for other schools.

For example, as reform progressed at Kennedy High, the assistant
superintendent spoke about the school's efforts at conferences, and
the board vice president spoke to board members from other districts
across the state. As a result, faculty members began to receive invitations to address faculties at other schools about the reform process,
their progress in block scheduling, and their overall approach to
addressing student needs. In taking care to present a balanced picture
of the difficulties and successes they experienced in instituting new
processes and employing new strategies in the classroom, faculty
members reflected and discovered more ways of instituting school
reform.

Schools, both small and large, that are involved with major
changes can use such visits to their advantage. In addition, faculty
speakers may receive honorariums for their visits and presentations.
Some teachers may find addressing other faculties difficult. However,
other teachers may be confident about making such presentations,
whatever the size of group they address. Most will become more
confident about their professional capacities as a result of presenting
their accomplishments in a professional manner. Faculty presentations exemplify Sparks and Loucks-Horsley's model of involvement
and carry it to a different level.

Summary

Researchers agree that professional development is vital to the
reform process, that it facilitates skill development, and that it enables
staff to focus on achieving long-term school goals (Tewel, 1991).
Schools can use a variety of means for delivering professional development, and faculty can experience many enhancing opportunities
for professional growth. The majority of professional developmental
activities focus on training and strongly support involvement and
individually guided development. Faculty members who attend conferences, visit other schools, or participate in other reform-related

experiences outside the school can share the knowledge they gain with the rest of the faculty at meetings and in presentations.

Professional development strategies can positively effect actions taken by school faculty in creating reform. Staff development, school visitations, and information sharing can broaden the faculty's knowledge of education and educational approaches as well as reform strategies. Through professional development, the faculty can develop the decision-making skills and self-trust required to solve their own problems. Outside facilitators or resource persons may be important, but ultimately success will be guided by those on-site. Formal and informal professional development activities can help the teaching staff learn together and help the school in its direction to become a community of learners.

In addition to professional development approaches and characteristics, support is crucial to the success of reform and reform-related professional development endeavors. Chapter 4 will take a detailed look at the role of support in reform and will address the importance for support of teacher, student, and community-wide decision making.

Involving Teachers, Students, and Community in Decision Making

Chapter Focus

Chapter 4 focuses on decision-making processes. The variety of approaches taken at different schools to shared decision making offer guidance to widening involvement in decision making about school-related issues. Involvement of faculty, parents, and students in decision making can support reform efforts. The more the responsibility for reform efforts is shared, the more ownership of results there will be.

Key Insights From the Literature About Shared Decision Making

A school organization is more effective when there is concern for meeting human needs. Participation and involvement in shared decision making are ways that individuals can be actively engaged and share a sense of responsibility for the school. With commitment and involvement, human needs and motives can be met. This is one way leaders can address the human resource frame as outlined by Bolman and Deal (1993). They found that when managers and leaders provide a caring, trusting work environment, the organization works best because of meeting individual needs. When school leaders rely on the human resource frame, they show concern and provide extensive opportunities for involvement, shared decision making, and active participation at all levels.

If not already established, a strong partnership that includes empowerment, enablement, and enhancement needs to be created with parents, teachers, and students (Sergiovanni, 1990). Empowerment is a sharing of authority that increases responsibility and accountability. Enablement means offering opportunities and removing obstacles so individuals can be successful. Enhancement is when the leader becomes a leader of leaders; that is, followers' roles are enhanced to increase commitment and high performance. Parents, as well as students, need to be invited to join the educators and shown how to participate in school governance so that the process of schooling improves. Principals who successfully reform schools bring people together as teams for shared decision making and empowerment (Blase & Blase, 1994). Shared leadership by teams results in better decisions, support for decisions, and improved morale. Teams need to focus on group well-being as well as achieving the desired outcomes.

Leaders should interact with group members in such a way as to evoke behaviors that contribute to achievement. According to Owens (1991), effective leadership is evidenced by followers who are motivated to do what leaders request because they find it rewarding and satisfying to do so. The participants are clear about the purposes of the organization and have reached agreement on mutual values. There is also a commitment to continuous growth and development for everyone in the organization, thus everyone is a learner.

People who believe they cannot influence their organizations feel restricted and victimized because they perceive that top management controls decision making. "Top-down management," according to Morhman and Lawler (1996), is hierarchical and control-oriented. This management style can be observed in school settings as restricted access to resources, decision making by an individual or a selective group of people, secretiveness, the withholding of information, and emphasis on formal roles. Reform efforts can help encourage a shift from top-down management styles to styles that include role expansion, increased motivation, and shared decision making. Expectations for success, involvement, and personal ownership motivate people to behave in ways that promote reform efforts. If people believe they can successfully achieve meaningful goals that will lead to intrinsic and/or extrinsic rewards, their energies can be harnessed in a positive manner.

Participation in the decision-making process by those affected directly or indirectly by the school improvement effort promotes success. Contextual factors can work to support or block efforts to improve school effectiveness. Critical inquiry into school strengths and weaknesses should be an ongoing and school-wide activity (Boyd, 1992). Participation in discussion and planning for change engenders greater commitment and a sense of responsibility for achieving change goals.

Participatory management is particularly effective when the focus is on teaching and learning, the heart of what schools are all about. When this is the topic, principals need to keep teachers involved, well informed, and focused on instructional issues. In short, the principal's role is to provide guidance and maintain the group focus when it comes to teaching and learning (Bernd, 1992).

Principals who want to promote a climate that is responsive to change must provide opportunities for teachers to work collaboratively to solve problems and develop new initiatives. In effect, "decisions that affect the teaching and learning process should be made as close as possible to the classroom" (Tewel, 1991, p. 17). Teachers should be included in decisions that affect their classrooms, especially regarding teaching and learning processes. Those involved in decision making must be equipped to participate effectively in this shared decision making.

Clear and consistent communication is also important for effective participation. However, communication skills are often taken for granted. Teachers traditionally work in isolation and have not developed these skills adequately. Not many school districts provide opportunities to learn more about skills for communicating among faculty members, let alone with parents and other community members. The National LEADership Network (Mojkowski, 1991) identified communication as a fundamental element in restructuring efforts. Yet, many schools typically confine communication to formal channels and restrict the substance of discussion to administrative requirements. In contrast, reform requires frequent information sharing and intensive faculty collaboration, which, in turn, calls for wider communication channels and greater opportunities for faculty interaction.

Shared Decision Making in Schools

In most schools, faculty participation marks the first significant shift away from top-down decision making. Student and parent involvement tend to follow. Ultimately, widespread involvement and shared decision making should become a driving force in reform efforts. Shared decision making means shared leadership and accountability for reform results. It tends to encourage full participation and to create greater levels of commitment among those involved. As discussed in earlier chapters, participation and commitment are fundamentally important characteristics of successful school reform.

The remainder of the chapter explores ways of promoting widespread involvement in shared decision making. Each key role group—teachers, students, parents, and community—is treated separately.

Faculty Participation in Decision Making

Faculty involvement in decision making is likely to occur when one or more of the following conditions prevail: a leader who wants to share decision making, an administrative directive, or an initiative from the state education agency. Ultimately, a group in a school, which might be referred to as the building management team, school improvement team, or change agent team, usually made up of the principal and teachers (serving as representatives from each department in a high school or representatives from each grade level in an elementary/middle school) will form the basis for faculty participation in decision making. The principal will be only one voice on the team if members function as equals in a participatory decision-making group. Successful teams hold regular, often weekly, meetings that promote constant communication and follow-up of any concerns or issues. It is helpful if these meetings are open sessions so that any faculty member can attend them. Actions that can be taken to increase teacher participation in decision making include the following:

1. Use of a variety of communication channels to increase faculty involvement in decision making; for example:
   a. Distribute management team minutes
   b. Display meeting records
   c. Use workshop sessions and faculty meetings to obtain input
2. Establish the management team as a collegial faculty and administrative group with decision-making powers
3. Focus the discussion on teaching and learning issues

Communication as a Means to Increase Involvement in Decision Making. Improving and expanding the flow of communication can increase the faculty's input in the decision-making process. Linda Darling-Hammond (1996) notes faculty communication about governance and change permeates high-performance schools both horizontally, across the faculty, and vertically, from faculty to students, administrators, and staff.

A variety of strategies can be used to maximize participation and maintain a whole-school perspective. First, before faculty involvement in decision making can take place in a troubled school, some degree of stabilization and some restructuring of teachers' negative expectations have to be put in place. As this happens, the school's building management team can begin to function as a decision-making body, and faculty members can begin to explore solutions to school problems. Rather than being arrived at and imposed by administrators, proposals and directives can flow back and forth between faculty and staff. Teacher input can directly affect decision-making outcomes, as faculty energies are turned toward important school-wide issues.

Second, to ensure that other faculty members have ample opportunity to understand, have input about, approve, and support their suggestions and decisions, the building management team will need to take concrete steps to communicate with and involve the faculty at large. This can be done in different ways. For example: The team can distribute and display meeting minutes and records in key school areas, and recommendations and decisions can be presented and discussed at faculty meetings. Regular two-way communication with the larger faculty can keep everyone involved with the team's activities. The clear message should be that there are no hidden agendas.

Even with specific actions to keep everyone informed, there is always room for improvement. For example, a Kennedy High faculty member's assessment of the management team's approach at that school acknowledged the team's efforts but pointed toward needed improvement:

> The faculty has been asked to give their input in all these matters. . . . They [building management team members] send out flyers to say what they have discussed, and they speak to us about some of the decisions they've made. So in that sense, they've done a very good job. Sometimes, though, a meeting is called, and some of us don't know what is going on. Communications can always be improved.

A member of the building management team agreed that "Communication can always be improved":

> [Flip charts of the meeting minutes] fill up the faculty lounge wall. If they're not out, faculty will ask, "Where's the paper from the meeting?" And we always put out the report of what we talked about and what was decided. It's typed up and distributed, usually within a day, through faculty mail. . . . If there's something really important, we'll announce it. But we try not to rely on announcements because, to be perfectly honest, in most of the rooms, you can't understand the intercom.

Although sending minutes through faculty mail, making announcements over the loudspeaker, and posting flip charts from meetings may appear to be basic communication techniques, such actions represent significant communication improvements in many schools. They require extra effort and an abiding commitment to faculty interaction and involvement. The building management team's approaches to communicating with faculty members can facilitate faculty-at-large participation and input.

The Building Management Team, a Decision-Making Group. A building management team does not just happen, it has to be established, developed, and nurtured. How the team is prepared through training to become a decision-making body is important. Equally important is which decisions become the responsibility of the building management team.

First, professional development workshop sessions and other activities, such as those suggested in Chapter 2, can promote collaboration and shared decision making within the team and between the team and the rest of the school faculty. People tend to assume that they know how to participate in making decisions and that participating in decision making requires little in the way of training or skill. On the contrary, participation in decision making should be treated as a shared learning process.

Because lack of understanding and experience pose real obstacles to effective staff involvement, additional training in site-based decision making and consensus building should be provided, at least for team members. Such training can play a key role in enabling a team to make the transition from a group of individuals, to an advisory group, and to a well-functioning decision-making body. Over time, a building management team can conduct effective meetings with efficient time management.

Management teams can become effective by promoting facilitative leadership. For example, at one school a meeting facilitator takes minutes and a meeting "taskmaster" maintains the agenda for each meeting. The group rotates these positions among members from one meeting to the next, thus ensuring that all members share responsibility equally for meeting coordination and focus. The strategy works. As one team member remarked,

> [The Assistant Superintendent] showed us how to do this [group decision making] in one quick afternoon, and we've been using it ever since. Now our meetings take less time and

we accomplish more. We all know what to expect and we know what was decided when we finish a meeting.

This member attributed the team's more effective functioning to the facilitation and decision-making skills gained with training. Another teacher said effectiveness is also extended through openness and encouragement of participation by others:

Decisions are made as a group. The team has weekly meetings and they're open, whoever wants to can come. . . . Our faculty is involved and [building management team members] ask for our input.

Second, on some occasions complex issues may arise that require more focused attention than the team at large can give. On these occasions, the team can form committees to examine the issue more closely and to develop suggestions for resolution. Faculty members other than those on the team should be encouraged to serve on these committees or at least to communicate their ideas or concerns about specific issues to team members. In fact, in early stages of reform, such participation can begin to move toward involvement of students, parents, and other community members.

Decision Making Focused on Instructional Issues. Too many demands on the team can result in its members becoming discouraged. The management team and its ad hoc committees or task forces should focus on particular tasks that need resolution, not all issues facing the school. Success in resolving a limited number of relevant issues can give team members confidence in their decision-making abilities and motivate them to take on greater challenges.

A second consideration is that participation can be extended if the focus is on educational issues. When issues relating to instruction come before the group, the team can encourage wider faculty involvement in decision making. This approach follows Tewel's (1991) recommendation to involve those closest to a decision's outcome in its formation. It also helps the group avoid "burnout" that results by taking on more issues than it can reasonably or effectively address.

To solicit faculty involvement in decisions about instruction, the management team can host before- and after-school faculty meetings. Team members can use these sessions to review the status of current issues, discuss options before arriving at a decision, and generate wider faculty commitment.

An example of a team's approach to working with the faculty to resolve an instructional issue is Kennedy High's development of an alternative school calendar. According to the district calendar, the fall semester ended prior to winter break. The building management team formed a committee to review the calendar and consider ending the semester after the holidays. The committee designed an alternative calendar and presented it to the faculty for consideration. The faculty supported the proposal, which was then reviewed and approved by the district-wide calendar committee and the board of education. The board adopted the calendar for the following school year and has continued to use it in the years since.

Other decisions made by a management team in consultation with the faculty include a revised exam schedule, an early dismissal schedule for the fall semester, and guidelines for physical education courses. Together, the team and the faculty at large established a benevolence fund, named a chairperson, and solicited volunteers to work on the school's master schedule and ninth grade curriculum. The team also addressed student and faculty concerns relating to the use of tardy bells, student enrollment late in the semester, students being called out of classes, testing conditions, library hours, and computer lab access.

Developed in conjunction with parent and community representatives, an alternative education program also made improvements to delivery of its academic curriculum and increased available opportunities for student success. The alternative program established a "school within a school," offering courses for repetition and extending school hours to provide time for intensive study. The alternative program was later formally named the Academy of Opportunity and has made a substantial positive impact on graduation figures. A program such as this can also generate more money for the district and the school, especially in states where funding is enrollment-based.

Opportunity to Plan Together and Solve Problems. As has been noted, opportunities for the faculty to plan together and to solve problems can present themselves in a variety of ways. First, the faculty can take the opportunity to discuss and solve problems during activities that are a part of their professional development experiences. Second, the management team can constantly solicit commitment, clarification, and understanding from the faculty through faculty meetings, distribution of minutes, and posting of their action on flip charts. By maintaining a continuous cycle of communication, the building management team ensures the entire faculty's involvement in decision making.

A block schedule can build more time into the school day for departmental and faculty meetings and so provide a third venue for faculty planning and problem solving. One block schedule, 4 × 4, provides teachers with an 85-minute planning period. The 4 × 4 schedule restructures the school day to include longer class periods and a breakfast break. Block scheduling's longer classes expand teaching opportunities beyond those typical of short period classes in which, too often, time is available only to present facts and test students to see if they can recall them. Longer classes give teachers and students time to examine topics in depth, making the curriculum both more interesting and more challenging. Block scheduling generally requires greater teacher commitment. Researchers recommend additional professional development as one means to prepare teachers for the demands of longer classroom time (Cushman, 1995).

Teachers also use the 50-minute lunch period to hold faculty meetings when information sharing needs to occur. Even a 30-minute breakfast break provides time for collaboration—small groups of faculty members sometimes use the morning break to discuss a particular student's progress or to identify a concern that needs more attention.

Another school's team revised the daily instructional schedule, the school-wide Title I program, and developed a weekly early dismissal in order to have common professional development time for the faculty. These changes are beginning to pay off with increased student achievement in language arts and math.

If reform is to occur, the staff and community must value and create the time to work together. Teachers need time to plan together.

Collaborative and shared decision making that includes parents and community with teachers and students takes time.

Involving Students in Decision Making

Encouraging student participation in decision making regarding issues that affect them directly is an important reform activity. Not only is it a way of treating students as people within the organization, it is a way of having students experience real-life problem solving. Methods for involving students may change from time to time, but might include sharing information and soliciting widespread student input about instructional, curricular, and other student-related issues such as extracurricular offerings and behavioral expectations or forming a student advisory group.

Student Input. Encouraging students' input can increase their participation in decision making. Fullan (1991), underscoring the importance of student participation in reform, notes that failure to pay attention to students' thoughts about specific changes that affect them has significant consequences:

> To say that students do not have opinions and feelings about these matters [innovations] is to say that they are objects, not humans. Those responsible for innovations would be well advised to consider explicitly how innovations will be introduced to students and how student reactions will be obtained at that point and periodically throughout implementation. . . . The more complex the change, the more that student involvement is required. (p. 189)

Opportunities for students to have input into decision-making processes will increase as teachers reach out to hear the "students' voices." For example, during faculty discussion about block scheduling at Kennedy High, a teacher asked what students thought about the idea. The principal asked teachers to talk with students about block scheduling and share responses with him. One teacher reported,

I've talked to a lot of my students and they seem very open minded about [block scheduling]. They feel very positive about this change. . . . Especially my lower ability students. They seem to like the idea. They feel they can hold it together for a semester.

A student remembers: "The counselors came into our English classes and asked us about what we wanted. . . . And some students voted in the English classes on the block schedule during my junior year." Although there was not an election for all students, many voiced their opinions and the English classes did have a vote on the matter of block scheduling.

Student involvement in decision making not only increases the likelihood of successful decision-making outcomes; it also promotes development of students' skills that will be useful throughout their lives. Students who learn to participate in their own education can go on to be more effective participants in areas that affect their well-being as adults. Decision-making skills learned at school can benefit them as they participate in their communities, their families, and their professional careers.

Student Advisory Groups. Most secondary schools have some type of student advisory group. For example, it might be composed of the Student Council, which can be elected by the student body and be representative of all grades, or it can be a group specifically chosen or elected for the purpose of involvement in reform efforts. However it is formulated, the group can be charged with discussing school issues and representing student needs and expectations. If possible, it is better to form a student advisory group that represents a cross-section of students. To achieve this representation, instead of student council members, there might be teacher-nominated or student-elected members from the student body. The advisory group can include students who are not actively involved in any school-related activities, as well as student athletes and representatives from school-sponsored activities.

Student advisory groups can be most effective when they are involved in decisions that affect students. For example, the student advisory group at Kennedy High discussed block scheduling and even had one of their members participate in exploring alternative school schedules. In addition, the student advisory chairperson accompanied a faculty team on a visitation to a school using block scheduling and reported his findings to the student group.

A student advisory group can be a good, solid first step in involving students in decision-making processes. As with other participants, providing training for the group in decision-making processes and participatory management can enhance the work of the group. During the first year of the block schedule, a student from Kennedy High commented:

> We used to ask, "Why don't you combine A and B lunches?" And they (administration and counselors) would say, "No, that would cause too many problems." . . . We also asked for longer passing periods . . . and they would say, "We can't." And finally this year they did give us the longer lunch period, they did combine the lunches, they did give us the ten-minute passing period. And it worked. We all like it. . . . [The principal] listens to us. He takes the time to listen. . . . Even the teachers . . . listen. . . . Before, they could care less. . . . We're asked about our opinion.

Involving Parents in Decision Making

As educators know, meaningful parental involvement in high schools is almost nonexistent. Student success is related to parent involvement; therefore, parents need to be involved so that students achieve academically at higher levels. Parents can also offer insights about students and the community that may not be apparent to the educators.

Parents respond to athletic programs, especially if they are successful, to acts of violence, and to "hot button issues," such as gay rights, prayer in schools, racial discrimination, or closed campus, but such participation tends to be short-lived and, too often, negative. Athletic programs and other student events bring parents to the school as observers, not participants. Active parent involvement in helping to examine or determine a high school's educational mission, goals, and activities is rare. High school dynamics themselves appear to discourage parent participation. Adolescents prefer that their parents not come to school, while parents of adolescents often want to give their teenagers increased independence—that is, room to make their own decisions.

As a result, lack of parental involvement is the reality in both small and large districts. In fact, as Fullan (1991) concludes, in most communities active participation in reform decisions about educational programs is rare. The majority of parents, Fullan argues, do not gain much meaning from participation in school-wide endeavors. Yet, he believes that almost any community has the potential for increased involvement in the change process. To tap this potential, he recommends that school leaders begin by articulating an explicit plan for parental and community involvement and assigning a person or group the responsibility for organizing and conducting specific activities to bring parents and school people together. To be effective, the plan should be geared toward developing knowledge and skills and should encourage teachers, students, parents, and other community members to focus on particular purposes or goals.

Approaches devised for involvement in decision making at schools include community forums, parent organizations, and governance councils. These approaches do not always achieve hoped-for results, but there are lessons to be learned through experience for improving approaches for the future. Overall, they create opportunities for learning more about the challenging nature of parental and community involvement. The faculty and administration can apply what they learn to other endeavors and to a clearer assessment of the roles of parents and community in education reform.

Parent Organizations. Parent organizations are widespread at the elementary level. Parents are frequently visible as volunteers in these schools. They raise funds for materials, computers, and field trips; assist with school activities such as special events or holiday parties; and purchase supplies and equipment for the school. High schools, on the other hand, may have active parent organizations, but they are limited in numbers and are much more likely to support limited purposes; for example, booster clubs for various sports or clubs and fund-raising for equipment or travel.

As an example of the difficulty of stimulating parental involvement, take the case of a high school principal who wanted to organize parents to be involved in decision making regarding the school as a whole. Even though only a few parents were willing to address such needs under the umbrella of a Parent-Teacher Organization, he set out to develop activities geared to enhance school pride and student spirit. Working with little support and putting in many hours to host student activities, the group ran out of energy by the end of its first year.

Unwilling to give up on his goal for increased parental involvement, the principal persisted by bringing in a representative from the Parent Teacher Association (PTA) from a neighboring district. The representative made presentations to parents, but they remained unwilling to affiliate themselves with a school PTA. One parent said a cultural wall separated them, and they wanted to be left alone to do their own thing. The principal dropped the idea, but did not give up on the goal. Although he hoped for participation from a large number of parents, he recognized the advantages offered by a few parents willing to devote quality time to school decision making. Instead, he sought ways to put that willingness to better use.

It is important to listen to parents regarding their interest in certain forms of parent organizations. School people may have a different perception of organizations that the culture of the community may not be interested in joining.

Community Forums. Community forums are meetings that are open to the community for the purpose of discussing school-related topics—they are much like town hall meetings. An agenda for discussion topics can be developed, with presentations made by school faculty on important issues. A question-and-answer session can follow to allow attendees to voice their opinions. The community forum should be designed to explain reform concerns and to provide opportunities to receive input from the larger community. School leaders can plan for and host evening community forums. These functions can be publicized through local newspaper advertisements, community radio announcements, and by word of mouth. Students can be given take-home flyers about the forums.

Parent response to such efforts varies. For example, at one high school all the best laid plans did not result in parent participation. As one teacher said,

> We tried to get the parents in here so we could tell them what
> we want to do, get their input and their concerns. I think at least
> a dozen of us, administrators, counselors and teachers, showed
> up. Not a single parent came, not one.

As might be expected, the faculty was disillusioned by the total lack
of parent participation. Faculty members who eagerly awaited parents for the evening discussion session were visibly frustrated when
parents did not show up.

At another school, however, community forums resulted in large
numbers of parents attending. Some parents even volunteered to be
facilitators after receiving training to play this role. Other parents took
responsibility for getting the word out about the sessions. Community
forums continue to be used at this school as a means of involving the
larger community in decisions regarding reform efforts and change.

These two examples illustrate how unpredictable it can be to
engage the community in school reform efforts. However, lack of
parental involvement may not be negative. It may indicate parent and
community trust rather than lack of interest. Perhaps they do not
attend meetings because they are basically in support of school personnel actions, and, therefore, put their energies elsewhere. Lack of
parent involvement in decision making does not have to deter school
reform progress, even though it may dampen faculty enthusiasm. In
addition, experience has made it clear that timing for community
forums is very important, especially if the function conflicts with other
community activities.

Governance Council. A governance council can give teachers, students, and parents meaningful representation in decision making. It
is a way to bring stakeholders to the same table to discuss reform
openly and engage in the decision-making process. A governance
council's purpose should be to improve teaching and learning radi-
cally for the benefit of all children and the community as a whole. In
turn, with a collaborative approach, schools can be more innovative
and accountable for the quality of instruction and for students' academic success (Swap, 1993). The group can be organized to reflect
accurately the ethnic balance of the student body; parents and students

can be selected to represent each class, and teachers can represent departments or grade levels. Ground rules for members of the council include maintaining confidentiality, honoring each other as equals, and voicing opinions freely. Members should be encouraged to bring their individual perspectives to the group to foster effective collaboration and problem solving.

At the elementary and middle school levels, students usually are not a part of the governance structure. The schools more often use a team approach to school improvement. Teachers and parents serve on a voluntary basis on the school management team. They maintain communication with the remainder of the school staff and parents.

Summary

All participants have a legitimate and important role to play in school reform. Faculty participation in decision making can be realized through techniques that target increased communication and involvement. Increased faculty communication and mechanisms for faculty input through departmental/grade level representatives can enable the faculty to be involved with the school management team in making decisions. The management team can encourage faculty involvement in decision making by promoting equality and basing decisions on data, research, and consensus.

Student, parent, and community involvement in decision making can be promoted through vehicles such as student advisory committees, governance councils, and a widespread commitment to sharing information and ideas with students and parents. Although parent and community participation may be sporadic, faculty and administrators need to make efforts to increase their involvement. The bottom line is that the involvement of teachers, students, parents, and community in decision making can signal a willingness and desire to tackle the difficult problems associated with school improvement.

5

Support for Change

Chapter Focus

Chapter 5 explores the importance of support in the forms of beliefs, time and energy, inputs, and legitimacy, as well as funding on reform efforts. After a brief review of literature about support for school reform, roles of internal (within the school) and external (outside the school) support groups for change in schools will be explored. Support from role groups such as faculty and administration, the board of education, and the state department of education can positively influence the reform process.

Reform efforts benefit from both internal and external support. Both forms of support can make initial reform efforts possible and also contribute to maintaining school reform as an ongoing process. Support for early reform efforts help the school achieve successful outcomes. In turn, these successes help win the school support for later initiatives.

Key Insights From the Literature About
Support for Change

Support for educational change at federal and state levels has been enacted with laws and regulations. Fullan (1991) observes that educational change supported by government agencies is not only complex but also dilemma-ridden. Decision makers at each governmental level tend to have different and limited understandings of reform and therefore may not influence reform in the most effective or positive manner.

This reality makes leadership and support at the local level even more critical for school reform (Sizer, 1992). Before reform can begin, the following leadership elements are important (Fullan, 1991):

1. Active initiation and participation

2. Pressure and support

3. Changes in behavior and beliefs

4. Challenges of the overriding problem of ownership (p. 91)

These elements are necessary for success because so many forces operate to maintain the status quo. In a study of high school shared decision making, L. Miller (1995) states, "When it comes to making significant changes in practice, it is the principal's leadership and vision that most often provide the essential push" (p. 1). Reform requires leaders who are willing to push gently and apply pressure to overcome obstacles to change that cannot otherwise be achieved.

A close connection with the superintendent and central office administrators is a benefit to principals. A principal who constantly keeps the superintendent informed of the school's direction and key issues most often will find the superintendent shares pertinent information, guidance, and support. The role of the principal becomes one of balancing independence and dependence, as well as autonomy and outside influence. Ideas and problems are taken to the superintendent early on so there is time for discussion, problem solving, resource identification, and possible adjustments based on information from the superintendent. The principal also has to balance the responsibility to those above and below the organizational hierarchy as well as constituent groups. When principals succeed with maintaining the balance, superintendents and central office personnel can be supportive of change efforts (Goldring & Rallis, 1993).

Internal Support for Change

Internal potential for support comes from faculty and administrative behaviors and beliefs that promote change. Both can display support for change in various ways. School and district administrators who actively sustain change at the school level can also provide a variety of internal supports.

Faculty Support for Change

Developing a faculty consensus in support of change is vitally important. An ethnographic study of eight charter CES member schools conducted between 1986 and 1990 found that, "In most of the schools there was not a consensus that fundamental changes in school structure or teaching practices needed to occur" (Muncey & McQuillan, 1993, p. 487). When consensus about the need for change is not present within a faculty, reform work toward change will almost always be futile. A school's principal can clear the way for faculty participation, and apply pressure, and offer support, but faculty members must agree that change is needed before they will participate in change efforts.

Faculty agreement that change is needed has to be established. The faculty has to have a desire to participate in school reform. One symbolic way of acknowledging agreement, if indeed there is one, is to have faculty members sign statements committing themselves to support a reform effort. This might best be done after involving the faculty in assessing the current status of the school and discussing the need for change.

The faculty can further define its desire for change in a written exercise conducted during professional development workshop activities. Such activities were conducted at one school where a faculty member wrote:

I would like to see our school improve for faculty and students. At this time faculty members do not have a good image of themselves. Students do not have clear objectives as to their outcomes. Students are not challenged in the classrooms (educationally).

Another faculty member wrote:

Improve the school:
  1. academically
  2. socially
Find ourselves—determine direction.

This faculty used their workshop sessions as a way of committing to working together to improve the school. There was a shared belief that change was needed. For example, one teacher stated:

I think there's a need for change here at the high school. . . . We need to become more inward looking to see how things are going in our own classrooms. And we need to make change there.

This school's faculty clearly desired to change the school's status quo. The faculty's expressed desire for change made it possible to converge, develop a common picture, and turn their attention, participation, and energy toward reform.

Administrative Support for Change

Administrative support for change is often expressed first by the school's principal and then by the district's central office administrators. A principal's words, actions, and decisions demonstrate a pledge to turn the school into a better place for learning and a better place to work. A principal can make the reform agenda a priority through a variety of initiatives.

Selecting New Staff Who Are Positive Toward Change. When openings occur in faculty positions at a school, the principal can seek new staff who are positive toward change. Faculty committees can assist in interviewing applicants. The interview process can engage applicants in discussion about innovative ideas so the committee can obtain a sense of the applicants' educational philosophy/platform. Between them, the committee and the principal can actively work to reduce possible negative influences new teachers might have on the school's faculty by looking for people who will make positive contributions to the school's faculty change efforts.

Having All Staff Participate in Building-Level Professional Development. The school principal should opt to have all faculty participate in professional development activities rather than selecting a core of faculty members or leaving it to voluntary choice to receive training. This decision and action is a push, but as Fullan (1991) notes, pressure can also function as a support for needed reform.

Encouraging Risk Taking. A principal can do much to encourage faculty to try new approaches and to value experimentation. The principal will first need to assure the faculty that mistakes and failures are not only acceptable, but are viewed as the reality when reform efforts are attempted. With permission to make mistakes, the staff are more likely to be willing to take risks and to explore new approaches in the classroom.

At one school, a teacher expressed her reaction to the new approach in positive terms:

> One of the things that they've allowed us to do here is experiment. And they've supported us in what we're doing . . . as long as we let them know. . . . I've gotten good support from administration when I've wanted to try something different.

Giving Teachers Permission to Make Mistakes. Principals can offer the faculty verbal support for testing a variety of ideas in the classroom and can encourage teachers to move beyond status quo practices. However, principals can do much more than merely give verbal support. They can actively seek a variety of resources. For example, one high school principal allowed science teachers to conduct classes outside the classroom; approved changes in classroom color schemes; and, at one teacher's request, purchased tables, instead of desks, for student use in the classroom.

Obtaining Necessary Resources for the Staff. School administrators can also seek monetary and resource support for reform efforts from the district's superintendent. Kennedy High School's principal sought and received the superintendent's approval for (a) expenditures for half of the tuition of faculty members who wanted academic credit for the local university professional development course; (b) monetary support for substitute costs when faculty visited other schools or attended professional conferences; (c) support for travel costs; and, when needed, (d) substitute coverage. In all, the district paid approximately $10,000 for substitutes, travel, and professional conferences for reform activities and for tuition costs.

Other district administrators can also become a direct resource for reform efforts, and, if there is a good relationship, principals will feel free to call on central office administrators for advice about reform ideas that are being considered. For example, district leadership can assist with planning and conducting professional development activities. Central office administrators may have needed expertise and experience that is not present at the school. They can also influence reform efforts by being unfailing allies to the principal.

An assistant superintendent at High Point District, Mary Gilbert, was an advocate for Kennedy High School faculty's actions when questions arose at the district office or at school board meetings. From firsthand experience, she would provide the background or details about the high school's reform efforts. For example, she assured the board that the faculty's examination of research about block scheduling was in-depth when the subject came up for board approval.

Although Assistant Superintendent Gilbert considered these actions a part of her professional responsibility, her commitment to Kennedy High School generally exceeded that displayed by most central administrators to schools in their districts. She was asked about ways of obtaining facilitation skills. She decided to provide training for the school's management team. She also selected articles that she thought would be useful and gave them to the principal for distribution to the faculty. She did not hesitate to offer assistance through any means available.

Principals should not hesitate to ask for support from central administration. If one does not ask, one will not know to what extent support can be provided. Partnerships for change between the school and district leaders can go farther than if principals struggle with reform on their own.

External Support for Change

External support for change includes individuals', groups', and organizations' decisions or occurrences that are peripheral to schools but can have a big impact on their reform efforts. External forces include parents, businesses and community agencies, universities, the state department of education and other state-level agencies, and the board of education. This section will focus on three external forces that can be engaged to support change: national reform initiatives, the state department of education and other state-level agencies, and the local board of education. Roles of parents and the larger community have already been discussed in Chapter 4.

National Reform Initiatives

External support for reform can come from national reform movements. Some of the national organizations that focus on reform include the Coalition of Essential Schools, Quality Schools, Accelerated Schools, Paideai, Roots and Wings, and Connect Schools (Henry & Milstein, 1997).

Such organizations can provide training, information about reform efforts in schools, and can identify networks of schools involved in reform. Participation in organizations dedicated to reform often is at a cost to the school or district, but sometimes reform organizations have grant funds to distribute to schools for professional development activities or curriculum development.

The first external support for Kennedy High School's reform efforts was in the form of a $5,000 grant from a foundation sponsoring school participation in the Coalition of Essential Schools. The funds were earmarked for professional development activities such as school visits, professional conference attendance, on-site consultants, substitutes, and extended contracts for summer planning and development activities. Substitutes freed some time for permanent faculty to visit other schools and attend professional conferences. Extended contracts allowed faculty members to develop the details of block scheduling, collaboratively plan an alternative education program, plan professional development activities for the coming year, and write needed curriculum. The principal maintained a close and collegial relationship with the funding source and solicited continued funding for the following year. As a result, the foundation increased the previous year's grant to $10,000. The next year, funding was provided for each of the district's schools.

The State Department of Education

External support can also come from the state department of education (SDE) and other state agencies whose policies and regulations encourage school district reform. Educators often view state agencies as regulators or guardians of the status quo and question whether they can actually play any positive role in reform efforts. This view overlooks the openness and encouragement that state agencies can uniquely offer. SDEs, by definition, must enforce compliance and accountability, but they can also lend assistance, demonstrate leadership, and seek legislative support for reform. Focusing only on the SDE's enforcement functions, educators too often underestimate its potential to offer a helping hand. For example, the SDE may define and enforce the required hours of instruction in a school year, the number of instructional days per year, required courses for high school graduation, curriculum standards at all grade levels, and pupil/teacher ratio patterns. But, the SDE also can promote school improvement programs. Most SDEs have a method to waive regulations for length of schoolday, staffing patterns, subject areas, or purchase of instructional materials. In other words, the SDE regulations contain within themselves enough flexibility to enable a school or local district to change the regulations. Thus, what an SDE may appear to take away with one hand, it may in fact offer with the other.

The SDE's accreditation process often shows similar flexibility and likewise contains within its restrictions room for schools and districts to make their own choices. Even the regional associations for accreditation, working closely with SDEs, advocate processes for schools to conduct a self-study; share the results with district personnel, parents, students, and community members; and use information from the study to design a school improvement plan. Such a plan must include clear expectations, implementation strategies, and an evaluation component. Schools may revise or adjust the plan, if needed. SDE requirements for accreditation themselves support school individuation, innovation, and change, and encourage schools to develop their own methods for improving student learning.

An SDE can also provide support in the form of funding. In many states, federal funds allotted to the SDE for National Goals 2000 are available to school districts for local reform. For example, High Point District sought and received National Goals 2000 support to initiate systemic reform throughout the district. Funding enabled each of the district's schools to conduct self-analysis and school-level action planning and to develop educational improvement plans. These funds paid for substitute teachers, teacher stipends, and professional development training. Thanks in large part to the SDE, the process of reform begun at Kennedy High School was spread to other schools in the district.

Board of Education

The district's board of education, as the community's official representative body, can provide an important source of external support. Board members can listen to reports on reform progress at regular board meetings as a way to confirm change and to indicate appreciation for reform. The school principal or a faculty group can make these reports to keep board members updated on activities and progress. Because they are officially a part of a board meeting, such reports make reform efforts more apparent and bring public awareness to the process of change. Positive news about school change efforts is a public relations approach that needs to be pursued by educators. With such regular feedback about change activities, it is more likely that board members will voice encouragement and support, visit the school, and attend workshop sessions and parent-faculty meetings. Board members should also be encouraged to attend faculty training sessions to observe the process in action. The presence of board members at the school can demonstrate their ongoing interest in and support for reform efforts and gives them firsthand knowledge of the school's achievements.

If board members are knowledgeable about a school's reform activities, it is more likely that they will encourage others to support the reform's progress. Because each board member has a circle of professional and social acquaintances with whom he or she can discuss reform efforts, word of mouth can become one of the best testimonies for a school. Of course, school faculty members will be encouraged and motivated to succeed by positive comments that are relayed back to them. Thus, recognition supports accomplishments and promotes continued reform efforts.

As an example, High Point's Board Vice President Vivian Jones seized every available opportunity to express her pride in Kennedy High School's reform activities. Her public support for the school's accomplishments helped increase the school's visibility and, ultimately, won it additional state-level support. As a fellow Goals 2000 committee member said to Vice President Jones, "Kennedy High School, Kennedy High School, everywhere I go, I hear Kennedy High School. There must be a lot going for Kennedy."

Assistant Superintendent Mary Gilbert also focused public attention on Kennedy High School's accomplishments. She spoke about the school at state-level conferences and meetings and, along with a federal programs coordinator, made presentations about district planning for changes at other schools based on the district's experiences at Kennedy High School. Kennedy's faculty appreciated the commitment and enthusiasm that Vivian Jones and Mary Gilbert brought to their discussions of Kennedy's achievements. As a result, they felt support for their own commitment and enthusiasm about reform efforts. Kennedy's faculty members knew that educators and others throughout the state were aware of their activities and that the school was becoming a model for reform. They took pride in the fact that success in their efforts meant not only improvements for Kennedy High School, but might also lead to similar improvements for other schools.

Summary

Support for change can come in a variety of forms. Possible negative influences can be mitigated when principals and faculty committees seek to hire new faculty members whose outlooks favorably support reform. Support can also be demonstrated when individuals, groups, and organizations outside the school actively involve and invest themselves in reform efforts. Superintendents and other central office administrators can help plan and implement professional development sessions and engage in support activities that take place outside the school. They, along with board members, can inform other participants at state-level meetings, make presentations to other districts, and communicate with officials and school administrators throughout the state. External support for change can also come through funding and resources, through recognition and investment from the board of education, and through financial and legislative assistance from the state department of education.

Support from within and outside of the school creates a safety net to keep the school's reform actions balanced and engaged. Each of these support sources provides further security for taking additional steps on the sometimes scary tightrope of change. Support plays an important role as the faculty gains a surer footing, assesses its current status, and looks toward continued improvement.

Synthesis and Transferable Lessons

Chapter Focus

This final chapter synthesizes the major points of Kennedy's story and explores implications for other school settings. First, key points made in Chapter 1 will be revisited and applied to the dynamics that occur in schools involved in reform to illustrate the importance of these aspects of school change efforts. The Kennedy High School case will be employed to develop these key points within a specific school setting. Second, thinking systemically, or putting it all together, will be emphasized. In this regard, a framework that can be used to guide school change efforts to encourage comprehensive change management, touching all the relevant bases along the way, will be depicted. Third, the importance of "staying the course" will be discussed. The focus on the change efforts introduced during the innovation stage needs to be maintained through the tough job of moving from initiating reform efforts to institutionalizing them at the school site.

Key Elements in Systemic Change

In Chapter 1, a typology by Sashkin and Egermeier (1992) was presented that identifies four different ways of going about changing schools—fixing the parts, fixing the people, fixing the school, or fixing the system. Assumptions that underlie the typology are that "fixing" one particular element is sufficient and that someone or some group can manage or "fix" the situation for the target group.

As the Kennedy case makes clear, situations that are comprehensive in scope require comprehensive change efforts. Focusing narrowly on one element or launching a time-bound, limited "project" is not likely to impact the situation more than superficially. Equally important, "fixing" suggests that the initiators and energizers of the change effort are doing something to or for others, which means they need to be outsiders—for example, the principal, central office administrators, university faculty members, or consultants. However, experience has repeatedly proven that, as was the case with Kennedy High School, solutions to problems invariably exist in the same group that is experiencing a problematic situation. Those who are caught up in the dissatisfactory state (i.e., "they are part of the problem") also have the potential ability to resolve it (i.e., "they are part of the solution"). They can access required information and, if motivated and given the tools required, are in the best position to make required changes. Given sufficient time, the development of readiness, adequate skill development, and the creation of safety nets that promote risk taking, members of the organization can engage in change initiatives more effectively than can well-meaning outsiders, even if the outsiders are "experts."

Turning around a large, ocean-going vessel takes moving the steering wheel one degree—and crossing about 15 miles of open water. This imagery helps put changing the large vessels we call schools into perspective. That is, significant change does not appear to happen immediately, but as the rudder is turned and starts to cut into the water, the ship will, in a relatively short space of time, turn around. We have identified several critical elements that have to be put in place to prepare for and manage the turnaround: setting the direction, professional development, involvement in decision making, support, and changing the culture.

Setting the Direction: Developing the Vision

The old saying, "You can't get there if you don't know where you are going!" holds true for school change. The extended dialogue that is needed before participants can come together to support a shared vision is not wasted time. Rather, it is the starting place for meaningful and successful change. An effective vision is one that leads to commitment, energy, and motivation; creation of meaning; establishment of standards of excellence; clarification of what a better future can look like; and transcendence of the status quo (Nanus, 1992). Further, the more a vision is debated and developed by those who will be expected to live by it, the more likely it is to be understood, accepted, and actively pursued by them.

Too often, there is a strong, urgent seeking after a "quick fix" that will minimize disruptions to routines. But, the cost of such fixes is significant. Usually, they lead to soon-to-be discarded, insufficiently thought-out responses to complex issues. Typically, frustration increases and belief in the ability to improve the situation decreases.

Early on at Kennedy High School, there was recognition of the need to formulate a shared vision. Early in the process, the faculty was introduced to the Nine Common Principles of the Coalition of Essential Schools (CES), which became the template for judging the status quo, guiding the development of appropriate educational experiences for students, and assessing the performance of educators. Once these principles were understood and agreed on, they became the basis for the development of goals and action plans. Similarly, the Student Advisory Committee explored normative expectations for behavior. The resultant Ten Rules for Success at Kennedy High School became the foundation for behavioral expectations for members of the school's learning community.

Both of these vision-setting documents were developed during the first year of the change effort. The principal and the faculty, through thick and thin, took the time needed to focus on intent before moving onto the action phases of change. Even now, the Kennedy faculty continues to revisit the vision. Such revisits serve partially to recommit and modify school-wide and classroom-based actions as needed, and partially to ensure that the school's new principal is clear and in agreement about the intent of the vision and, as important, committed to facilitating the pursuit of the goals associated with it. An added outcome of the continuing focus on vision is that the faculty has been able to respond effectively to the state department of education's push for districts to pursue comprehensive educational improvement plans.

Professional Development

Changing educational programs effectively cannot happen by dictate. Unless educators understand and agree with proposed modifications and have the skills and knowledge required to implement them, little is likely to change. As Lawson and Briar-Lawson (1997) remind us, appropriate and effective professional development for teachers must be provided if we realistically expect to improve student outcomes.

"Appropriate and effective professional development" initiatives are those that (a) avoid one-shot experiences, especially those that emphasize information without opportunities for internalization, because they rarely lead to any cumulative impact; (b) focus on skills and attitudes as well as knowledge; (c) recognize that complex change efforts require multifaceted developmental activities that are sensitive to different learning styles; and (d) promote the development of learning communities that provide opportunities to share ideas and develop strategies to facilitate collaboration.

Kennedy High School's principal met with significant resistance to his initial push for professional development activities, partly because there was no supportive culture for such efforts and partly because the emerging vision was not yet understood, let alone agreed on by faculty members. However, as the vision became clearer and more personal to the faculty, the urgent need for increased and improved professional development efforts also became more apparent. The kind of professional development opportunities provided by the district closely paralleled the major guidelines noted above: multifaceted activities, including partnering with the local university, which provided academic credit for participants; use of faculty meetings to promote dialogue and discussion about the vision and action plans; workshops that focused on the Nine Common Principles of the CES; teachers being sent to visit other schools engaged with CES initiatives; professional reading and discussion around priority instructional topics; identification and securing of internal and external fiscal resources to drive the effort; and prioritization of time needed for planning activities through before- and after-school meetings as well as through released time with substitutes being provided.

Besides providing the necessary structure and support to facilitate the reform, these efforts also sent a strong message throughout the system that professional development is an important foundation for the creation and implementation of a shared vision. They also sent the message that the system cares about its members and their ability to be successful at what they do. Ultimately, such professional development initiatives constitute the means by which learning communities are created, which is an important outcome that is above and beyond implementation of the change effort itself.

Involvement in Decision Making

As noted in Chapter 1, involvement in decision making by role groups that will be affected—students, parents, and other community members, as well as educators—is an important factor in successful change. This is true partly because involvement has the potential of improving the quality of decisions, and partly because it can improve satisfaction, enhance motivation, and lead to internalized commitment to the outcomes of these decisions. As individuals and groups share the experience of making decisions and initiating and implementing improvements, resistance to systemic change can also be reduced.

However, these outcomes will not automatically result from efforts to increase participation in decision making. Two cautions in particular are worth noting. First, the *content* of what is being decided is an important issue. If it is limited to governance—for example, who gets to decide, how communication will flow, what structures will be developed—the outcomes will probably have little impact on educational outcomes. The dialogue must center on educational *processes* (curriculum and instruction) and *outcomes* (academic achievement and preparation for the world of work and/or higher education). Second, people have to have a sense of "ownership" of the initiatives being proposed in order to take the time to dialogue and make decisions together. In the final analysis, we pay attention to things that we believe are important to us or to others we care about. What complicates matters is the fact that different role groups are motivated by different agendas.

At Kennedy, each role group responded differently to the urgings of the principal to become part of the decision-making process. Faculty members showed initial resistance because they were not sure they wanted to take the risks associated with changing their routines and patterns. Early efforts to involve them through an advisory committee resulted more in venting of frustrations than in positive engagement with change. Subsequent efforts were more successful, partly because the rules and structure shifted from an advisory group to a site-based management team, which has much more influence over decision making. Further, *all* faculty members have been encouraged to become involved in decision making through multiple avenues, including workshops and faculty meetings.

Students also are increasingly engaged in some aspects of the decision-making process. The initial effort was limited to an advisory group composed exclusively of student council representatives. This group was later superseded by an advisory group that includes representation of the total student body. In addition, teachers regularly share reform plans in classroom situations and bring student points of view to the table when teachers and administrators explore these plans.

Parent and community input has been more problematic. Established vehicles, such as booster clubs and the PTO, have not been effective as platforms for involvement in systemic change. Nor have new initiatives, such as community town hall meetings. This dilemma, which has been identified and chronicled in many other places, seems to be rather intransitive. In fact, as Fullan (1991) reminds us, most communities rarely become actively engaged in change decisions related to educational programs. This is particularly true at the high school level, where parent and community disengagement is most frequently at its highest. However, as noted in the Kennedy High School situation, community involvement tends to increase when there is some "hot button" issue or situation that engages the interest of community members (e.g., getting to know the new Kennedy principal, what he stands for, and what he intends to do).

Managers of change efforts need to recognize this reality and develop strategies for community involvement that are specific, focused, and clearly communicated in ways that tap into community members' motivational interests. There are many ways of going about this: for example, promoting volunteerism (e.g., to raise funds or to serve as aides or teachers); involving parents in student recognition events; developing workshops aimed at parental interests (e.g., stress management or parenting skills); home visits by teachers; making resource materials available for parents to use with their children; providing "take home technology"; reserving a parent room at the school that can be used by parent-aides or other volunteers; periodic phone calls by teachers to parents; early morning sessions for fathers ("Doughnuts for Dads") before they go to work; providing social service referrals; and developing a system of parent buddies to encourage new parents to participate in activities (Warner, 1994). There is, of course, no one best way to go about this important activity. Each situation calls for its own unique mix of activities. Whatever the approach or combination of approaches, the payoff, in the form of participation and support, can make the effort highly worthwhile.

Support

Educational change does not happen because of good intentions alone. The comprehensive reforms that are necessary inevitably require significant levels of support. As Wood (1995) notes, support needs to be viewed in the widest possible manner, including recognition and reinforcement, opportunities to share insights and problems and to learn from and with others, as well as the more commonly understood meaning of support—money and materials. Further, the support must come from peers as well as experts and authority figures if group members are going to be willing to leave secure places to take the risks that inevitably accompany important changes.

At Kennedy High School, there was recognition of the need to develop a multifaceted support base. *Peer support* came in the form of knowing that all faculty members were expected to participate in the effort. They all signed commitment statements and shared their expectations for outcomes. *Administrative support* was provided at all levels: The principal provided professional development opportunities for all faculty members, shared his views of what instruction might look like as a result of the effort, and encouraged experimentation without fear of retribution. The assistant superintendent spear-headed many of the planning activities, provided for and led work-shops, and identified professional readings to promote faculty members' engagement and dialogue. The district superintendent provided 50% of the tuition costs for teachers who wanted higher education credits, and reserved funds for substitutes when faculty members were engaged in reform activities. The *school board* requested regular feedback about the reform efforts and some board members made a point of visiting the school to see how things were progressing. Board members provided verbal support and encouragement in the community and on a state-wide level. Externally, the restructuring organization that provided support had staff members who monitored the reform effort closely and responded to requests for consultation, while the *state education department* provided necessary waivers, connected the faculty with other schools that could benefit from their experiences, and encouraged the school to use its reform priorities as the basis for responding to the state's requirement for a comprehensive plan for student success.

As Wood notes, support should provide opportunities to share insights and problems and to learn from and with others. Sharing and learning promote understanding, commitment, and a sense of being part of something bigger than oneself. However, to have this happen, participants need to engage in *regular assessment of progress*. Assessment can help to "set standards, create instruction pathways, motivate performance, provide diagnostic feedback, . . . evaluate progress, and communicate progress to others" (Herman, Aschbacher, & Winters, 1992, p. 2).

Assessment is an activity that is too frequently ignored or done superficially. At Kennedy High, for example, while the faculty has always conducted traditional academic assessments of student performance in the classroom, they are only now beginning to consider assessment of the systemic changes that have been instituted. While it is better to be late to assess than not to assess at all, it is important to initiate assessment activities as early as possible in systemic change efforts so that information regarding problems and progress can be shared and used to guide decision making.

Effective assessments should (a) focus on purposes (i.e., are we moving toward our goals?); (b) test things that are important to the participants (e.g., expectations for academic performance); and (c) motivate participants to be involved rather than penalize them for risk taking. To promote these assessment priorities, it is probably best to employ assessment instruments that are designed by participants rather than to rely on norm-referenced tests, unless such tests are directly related to systemic change objectives. It is also a useful practice to employ multiple assessment tools, because no one tool (e.g., test, observation, or interview) is likely to provide complete and comprehensive assessment information.

Support, in short, is the glue that is needed to hold systemic changes together. Support must come in many forms and from many sources. Participants in the process of change need to know that others want them to succeed and will support them in the effort in any and all ways that they can.

Think Culture, Not Project

Systemic change is not really about introducing some specific modification or some new thing. Nor is it about a single element—for example, governance, participation, structure, curriculum, or instruction. Rather, at a deeper level it is about changing the culture of the school—its beliefs, priorities, practices, preferences, and norms. It is well documented that schools are extremely resistant to change, in large part due to deeply embedded cultures that impede reform efforts (e.g., Bolman & Deal, 1993; Conley, 1997; Cunningham & Gresso, 1993). Organizational culture is equivalent to a mind-set that permeates an organization and results in dominant patterns of member behavior (Krug, 1992).

This mind-set can lead to rigidity and resistance to systemic change, as it initially did in the Kennedy High School situation. The resistance encountered during the first year of the effort was due, in large part, to the probability that routines and accepted norms would be disturbed. It took repeated efforts, coming from different vantage points, before the principal and the assistant superintendent began to make noticeable inroads into unfreezing the status quo (Lewin, 1947) in ways that permitted the introduction of necessary change initiatives. The mechanisms they used included developing a vision, promoting professional development, creating avenues for involvement in decision making, and providing various forms of support for the change effort. It took all of these mechanisms, cumulatively, to begin to chip away at the resistant culture that had developed over the years.

Promote Transformational Leadership

This "chipping away" is an aspect of "transformational leadership" (cf. Fullan, 1991; Yukl, 1994). As noted in Chapter 1, Professor Higgins could not have *created* a lady out of Eliza Doolittle if she did not already have the required qualities within her. What he did do was help her transcend or transform herself into what she had been capable of becoming all along.

What transformational leadership is all about is helping others do as Professor Higgins did with Eliza Doolittle. Like Professor Higgins, what transformational leaders do is facilitate processes whereby others are able to be what they were capable of being all along. The same basic raw materials exist before and after a systemic change effort. What is different is the changes in attitudes, skills, available information, motivation, and the group's willingness to take risks.

Transformational leadership is about facilitating others, helping them let go of the status quo situation and the "can't do" attitudes that permeate our school cultures. It is about challenging current beliefs and perspectives and encouraging experimentation with alternative beliefs and perspectives that promote growth, development, and success.

Putting It All Together

There are two concepts that can help guide successful systemic change. The first is, *be sure to cover all the bases* by attending to all of the elements that impact the reform. The second is, *stay the course.* Nothing of significance occurs until the change effort survives the vicissitudes of time. Moving from innovation to institutionalization—that is, when the change becomes an accepted way of life of the system—is what separates the many failed school change efforts from the relatively few that take hold and become the new status quo.

Cover All the Bases

Having a common perception of *what* needs to be done, *why* it needs to be done, and *how* it is to be done helps everyone involved stay focused. Although many participants may have a good sense of the vision—*the what (the substance) and the why* of the reform effort— few are likely to have a good grasp or sense of the *process* of change, let alone the elements that are part of that process. Leaders and participants need to understand the processes that are involved in systemic change and then monitor these activities to be sure they are used in the effort.

This book has emphasized the need to set directions, provide professional development, promote wide involvement in decision making, and ensure support for change. All of these activities are aspects of systemic change that are embedded in the framework presented in Figure 6.1. This framework, which can be used as a convenient checklist, is a broad perspective that can help guide systemic change efforts. Whether using the framework presented in Figure 6.1 or another that may be better understood by a particular group of participants, these elements need to be introduced early for reference purposes early in systemic change efforts.

The focus of the framework is on educational equity and excellence. All decisions regarding the change process should be made on the basis of the probable impact on these outcomes. To achieve these outcomes, there are four major elements in the framework—*purposes, structures and roles, beliefs and behaviors, and resources.* Each, in turn, is composed of four subelements (Milstein, 1993):

1. *Purposes* must be examined, modified, and clarified:
   a. The *mission* of the school district and the schools within it need to be examined and, as necessary, altered to reflect the changing realities of our shrinking world.
   b. Clearly stated and agreed upon *goals* that support the mission and provide clarity and direction for restructuring [hereinafter referred to as *systemic change*] efforts must be developed.
   c. *Long-term perspectives* of 5 to 10 years and the patience to stay the course through the inevitable lean times are required to

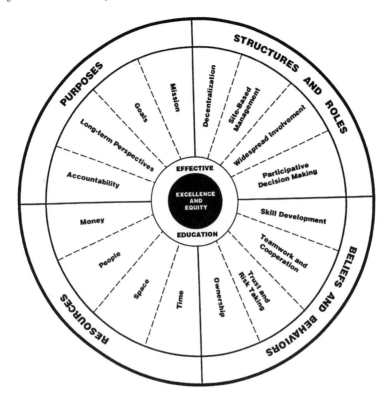

Figure 6.1. Elements in Restructuring A School

increase the potential of institutionalizing [systemic change] efforts. [We will return to this important point in more depth later in the chapter.]

    d. *Assessment and accountability* systems must be created and implemented to provide evidence of movement toward goal achievement and to remind those who participate about their responsibilities to monitor outcomes.

2. *Structures and roles* must be altered in ways that promote the achievement of purposes.

    a. *Decentralization,* a significant reduction of state-level oversight of school district activities as well as school district oversight of school-level activities, has to be implemented. The intent is to remove bureaucratic restrictions and hierarchical controls, both of which tend to inhibit motivation, ownership, and creativity at the school-site level.

  b. *Site-based management* must be pursued so participants will have opportunities to come together to sort through the school's needs and to develop creative responses to them.

  c. *Widespread involvement* opens the way for meaningful contributions by key groups, including teachers and other school-site personnel, parents and other community members, business leaders, and students.

  d. *Participatory decision making,* combined with the other structural changes, can lead to a sense of empowerment.

3. Specific *beliefs and behaviors* must be promoted to help everyone involved clarify and modify expectations and become more skilled and effective in achieving missions and goals.

  a. *Skill development* has to be promoted to enhance the potential of effective interactions. These skills relate to *governance* (e.g., goal setting, problem solving, meeting management, and conflict management) and to *effective education* (e.g., curriculum development; classroom management; and instructional delivery that supports concepts such as the teacher as coach and the student as worker, higher-order thinking skills, and cooperative approaches to learning).

  b. *Teamwork and cooperation* must be promoted because creative approaches to effective education are more likely to be forthcoming through cooperation than through competition.

  c. *Trust and risk taking* need to be promoted as empowerment is pursued through participation and cooperation.

  d. *Ownership* must be promoted so that all partners see the process as a win-win situation and [systemic change] efforts can take hold.

4. *Resources* must be identified and allocated to provide necessary support for the effort:

  a. *Money* is needed for a variety of activities, including skill development, curriculum development, alternative instructional delivery systems, and participatory management arrangements.

b. Because *people* ultimately make [systemic change] work, staff, students, parents, and other community members have to be motivated to participate in the effort as cooperative partners.

c. *Space* may need to be added, or at least modified, to promote changes in governance structures and instructional delivery systems.

d. *Time* is needed for participants to meet to agree on purposes, establish plans, put them into operation, and monitor outcomes. (pp. 5-7)

Turning schools around may leave the reader feeling a bit overwhelmed by the complexity of the effort and the commitments it seems to involve. This would be true if the tasks involved fell on one person's shoulders. However, if leadership is viewed as a shared function that must be performed effectively for the well-being and success of the group, then tasks associated with the elements in the framework should be perceived as the responsibility of the group, not of an individual. Many hands, heads, and hearts can do many things. It is important for formal leaders to delimit and contain their organizational roles by sharing initiatives with others. It is also important for participants in the process—teachers, other employees, parents, community members, and students—to be empowered as equal participants in the process. It is the only practical way to initiate and implement systemic change. Further, it is a way of modeling what an energized, healthy organization can look like and how it can function.

Stay the Course!

Innovating is one thing. Institutionalizing is quite another. Schools have been the focus of endless reforms, ranging from structural changes and procedural modifications, to curricular and instructional modifications. Very few of these reform efforts have become embedded in the life of schools. In part this is because of the homeostatic nature of organizations, particularly of school organizations, which has the effect of retarding any lasting effects, or even a residual of attempted changes, after a relatively short period of time. "This too shall pass" has become the catch phrase of many seasoned educators who find themselves being asked, yet again, to adapt to something different.

Innovation can be an attention grabber. It involves learning new things or new ways, taking some risks, joining others in taking on challenges, and being encouraged to be creative. Institutionalization, on the contrary, is more complicated and often more methodical than exciting. It centers on activities such as tightening policies, writing guidelines and rule books, repeatedly communicating the vision and goals, socializing new members, and coping with resistance.

Not surprisingly, many participants lose enthusiasm, if not interest, in the changes being addressed when the process shifts from innovation to institutionalization.

Yet, we know that institutionalization, or making changes stick until they become parts of the predictable way of life for the organization, is what matters. We also know that institutionalization takes more time—as much as 5 to 10 years for significant systemic change to take hold (Fullan, 1991)—than participants who want reforms to be implemented rapidly have the patience to endure.

That is why it is so challenging to stay the course. However, if leaders and participants understand that healthy organizations have to be in an ongoing state of renewal, institutionalization becomes more likely. The old saying, "The only constant is change" is true because environments change, organizational goals change, members leave and new ones join, technology improves, and resources grow or shrink. As these inevitable changes occur, organizations have to adapt, or they will soon become obsolete.

Institutionalization is complex and comprehensive. Basic requirements include focused attention on *development of a healthy organization* and a bias toward an *organizational renewal culture*. Healthy organizations are *always* undergoing systemic change. They recognize that they have to invent ways of responding to both external and internal changes. If participants come to recognize that organizations must respond to these challenges or fall behind in realizing their visions and goals, and are made aware of the costs associated with falling behind, efforts will be made to promote ongoing systemic renewal. Healthy organizations do not limit themselves to responding to crises by tinkering with change and getting on with their tasks. Rather, they think systematically and understand the need for regular focus on renewal.

An organizational renewal culture is one that promotes introspection, responsiveness, adaptability, and growth. It encourages close monitoring of systemic change efforts by regular diagnosis of progress, identification of necessary organizational modifications, and promotion of development activities for participants. It also encourages members to mark movement toward goal achievement by stopping to celebrate successful steps along the way.

Problems need to be confronted and responded to before they grow into intractable dilemmas, but long-term goals also need to be kept in front of participants as a reminder of agreed-upon compacts and the importance of recognizing short-term movements—markers and yardsticks—that are accomplished as they move toward long-term goals. Organizations that recognize the importance of practicing these renewal behaviors on a regular basis are much more likely to see the seeds of innovations blossom into institutionalized practices.

In Closing

School reform is a challenging task. Systemic change requires waking up the sleeping giant, getting its attention, motivating it to take pride in itself, helping it to be able to accept the challenges required to attain meaningful goals, and providing recognition for the efforts made and the outcomes attained. What is required is to bring leaders who care and understand that leadership is about doing what is needed to achieve important visions and goals; participants who accept the challenge to engage in the process; human and fiscal resources that enable all participants to acquire skills, become knowledgeable, and modify behaviors and attitudes; a focus on embedding the vision, goals, and reform activities in the organization's culture; and the tenacity to overcome the problems and obstacles until desired changes become institutionalized.

Systemic change is not for the faint-of-heart. It is the antithesis of the fix-it-quick, Band-Aid™ approach to change that is the approach taken in many schools. It is doubtful that the Band-Aid approach ever really worked, but certainly it does not now, nor will it in the future. The challenges that confront schools and their communities as they move into the 21st century require them to reconceptualize what they do and how they do it in ways that may not be at all apparent at the outset.

Appendix

The Nine Common Principles of the
Coalition of Essential Schools

1. Intellectual Focus
   The school should focus on helping young people develop the habit of using their minds well.

2. Simple Goals
   The school's academic goals should be so simple that each student can master a limited number of essential skills and areas of knowledge.

3. All Children Can Learn
   The school's goals should apply to all students, while the means to these goals will vary as those students themselves vary.

4. Personalization
   Teaching and learning should be personalized to the maximum feasible extent.

5. Student as Active Learner
   The governing practical metaphor of the school should be student-as-worker, teacher-as-coach rather than the more familiar metaphor of teacher-as-deliverer-of-instructional-services, student-as-passive-learner.

6. Authentic Assessment
   Teaching and learning should be documented and assessed with tools based on student performance of real tasks.

7. Tone
   Families should be vital members of the school community. Close collaboration between home and school yields respect and understanding.

8. Staff as Generalists
   The principal and teachers should perceive themselves as generalists first (teacher and scholars in general education) and specialists second (experts in one particular discipline).

9. Time and Budget
   Ultimate administrative and budget targets should include substantial time for collective planning by teachers, competitive salaries for staff, and an ultimate per pupil cost not to exceed that at traditional schools by more than 10%. (Sizer, 1992)

Tenth Common Principle

10. Democracy and Equity
    The school should demonstrate nondiscriminatory and inclusive policies, practices, and pedagogies. It should model democratic practices that involve all who are directly affected by the school. The school should honor diversity and build on the strengths of its communities, deliberately and explicitly challenging all forms of inequity and discrimination.

Principles 1–9 adapted from Sizer (1992).
SOURCE: Principle 10 reprinted with permission from the Coalition of Essential Schools, Inc., Vol. 14, No. 3, January, 1998.

References

Arnold, G. (1995, Fall). Teacher dialogues: A constructivist model of staff development. *Journal of Staff Development, 16*(4), 34-38.

Arterbury, E., & Hord, S. M. (1991). Site-based decision making: Its potential for enhancing learner outcomes. *Issues About Change, 1*(4), 1-8.

Barth, R. (1990). *Improving schools from within.* San Francisco: Jossey-Bass.

Beer, M., Eisenstat, R. A., & Spector, B. (1990, November-December). Why change programs don't produce change. *Harvard Business Review, 68*(6), 158-166.

Berliner, D. C. (1997). Voice training. *UCEA Review, 37*(2), 1, 9, 11, 14-15.

Bernd, M. (1992, January). Shared decision making requires effective instructional leadership. *NASSP Bulletin, 76*(546), 64-69.

Blase, J., & Blase, J. R. (1994). *Empowering teachers.* Thousand Oaks, CA: Corwin.

Bolman, L. G., & Deal, T. E. (1993). *The path to school leadership.* Newbury Park, CA: Corwin Press.

Boyd, V. (1992). *School context: Bridge or barrier to change?* (Office of Educational Research and Improvement Contract No. RP 1002003). Austin, TX: Southwest Educational Development Laboratory.

Cawelti, G. (1997). *Effects of high school restructuring: Ten schools at work.* Arlington, VA: Educational Research Service.

Characteristics of effective staff development activities. (1991, April). *National Staff Development Council,* p. 5.

Charters, W. W., & Jones, J. E. (1973). On the risk of appraising non-events in program evaluation. *Educational Researcher, 2*(11), 5-7.

Cohen, D. K. (1995). What is the system in systemic reform? *Educational Researcher, 24*(9), 11-17, 31.

Conley, D. T. (1997). *Roadmap to restructuring: Charting the course of change in American education.* Eugene, OR: ERIC Clearinghouse on Educational Management, University of Oregon.

Corcoran, T., & Goertz, M. (1995). Instructional capacity and high performance schools. *Educational Researcher, 24*(9), 27-31.

Cunningham, W. G., & Gresso, D. W. (1993). *Cultural leadership.* Boston: Allyn & Bacon.

Cushman, K. (1995, November). Using time well: Schedules in essential schools. *Horace, 12*(2). Providence, RI: Brown University, Coalition of Essential Schools.

Darling-Hammond, L. (with Chajet, L., & Robertson, P.). (1996). Restructuring schools for high performance. In S. Fuhrman & J. O'Day (Eds.), *Rewards and reform* (pp. 144-192). San Francisco: Jossey-Bass.

Darling-Hammond, L., & Goodwin, A. L. (1993). Progress toward professionalism in teaching. In G. Cawelti (Ed.), *Challenges and achievements of American education* (pp. 19-52). Alexandria, VA: Association for Supervision and Curriculum Development.

Dunlap, D., & Schmuck, P. (1995). *Women leading in education.* Albany, NY: SUNY Press.

Elmore, R. F. (1995). Structural reform and educational practice. *Educational Researcher, 24*(9), 23-26.

Fullan, M. G. (1993a). *Change forces: Probing the depths of educational reform.* London: Falmer.

Fullan, M. G. (1993b). Innovation, reform, and restructuring strategies. In G. Cawelti (Ed.), *Challenges and achievements of American education.* Alexandria, VA: Association for Supervision and Curriculum Development.

Fullan, M. G. (1996). Leadership for change. In K. Leithwood, J. Chapman, D. Corson, P. Hallinger, & A. Hart (Eds.), *International hand-*

book of educational leadership and administration (pp. 701-722). Dordrecht, The Netherlands: Kluwer Academic.

Fullan, M. G. (with Stiegelbauer, S.). (1991). *The new meaning of educational change* (2nd ed.). New York: Teachers College Press.

Glickman, C. (1991). Pretending not to know what we know. *Educational Leadership, 48*(8), 4-9.

Goldring, E., & Rallis, S. (1993). *Principals of dynamic schools.* Newbury Park, CA: Corwin.

Hallinger, P., & Richardson, D. (1988). Models of shared leadership: Evolving structures and relationships. *The Urban Review, 20*(4), 229-245.

Henry, D. A., & Milstein, M. M. (1997, January). *Restructuring models and their capacity for resiliency building.* Paper presented at the Tenth International Congress for School Effectiveness and Improvement, Memphis, TN.

Herman, J. L., Aschbacher, P. R., & Winters, L. (1992). *A practical guide to alternative assessment.* Alexandria, VA: Association for Supervision and Curriculum Development.

Hord, S. M. (1992). *Facilitative leadership: The imperative for change* (Office of Educational Research and Improvement Contract No. RP 91002003). Austin, TX: Southwest Educational Development Laboratory.

Keith, N. Z. (1996). A critical perspective on teacher participation in urban schools. *Educational Administration Quarterly, 32*(1), 45-79.

Kirst, M. (1991). Pitfalls to restructuring. *EDCAL, 20*(24), 1.

Krug, S. E. (1992). Instructional leadership: A constructivist perspective. *Educational Administration Quarterly, 28*(3), 430-443.

Lawson, H., & Briar-Lawson, K. (1997). *Connecting the dots: Progress toward the integration of school reform, school-linked services, parent involvement and community schools.* Oxford, OH: Danforth Foundation and Institute for Educational Renewal at Miami University.

LeCompte, M. D., & Dworkin, A. G. (1991). *Giving up on school: Student dropouts and teacher burnouts.* Newbury Park, CA: Corwin.

Lee, V. E., & Smith, J. B. (1994). High school restructuring and student achievement. In *Issues in restructuring* (pp. 1-5, 16). Madison: University of Wisconsin, Center on Organization and Restructuring of Schools.

Leithwood, K. A. (1992). The move toward transformational leadership. *Educational Leadership, 49*(5), 8-12.

Leithwood, K. A., Tomlinson, D., & Genge, M. (1996). Transformational school leadership. In K. A. Leithwood, J. Chapman, D. Corson, P. Hallinger, & A. Hart (Eds.), *International handbook of educational leadership and administration: Part II* (pp. 785-840). Dordrecht, The Netherlands: Kluwer Academic.

Lewin, K. (1947). Frontiers in group dynamics. *Human Relations, 1*, 5-41.

Lewis, A. (1997). A new consensus emerges on the characteristics of good professional development. *Harvard Education Letter, 13*(3), 1-4.

McLaughlin, M. W. (1990). The Rand Change Agent Study revisited: Macro perspectives and micro realities. *Educational Researcher, 19*(9), 11-16.

Miller, E. (1995). Shared decision-making by itself doesn't make for better decisions. *Harvard Education Letter, 11*(6), 1-4.

Miller, L. (1995, November 8). Focus on student learning is key in school restructuring, study says. *Education Week*, p. 6.

Milstein, M. M. (1993). *Restructuring schools: Doing it right.* Newbury Park, CA: Corwin.

Mitchell, D. E., & Tucker, S. (1992). Leadership as a way of thinking. *Educational Leadership, 49*(5), 30-35.

Mohrman, S. A., & Lawler, E. E., III. (1996). Motivation for school reform. In S. H. Fuhrman & J. A. O'Day (Eds.), *Rewards and reform* (pp. 115-143). San Francisco: Jossey-Bass.

Mojkowski, C. (1991). *Developing leaders for restructuring schools* (Office of Educational Research and Improvement, Leadership in Educational Administration Development Program). Washington, DC: National LEADership Network.

Muncey, D. E., & McQuillan, P. J. (1993, February). Preliminary findings from a five-year study of the coalition of essential schools. *Phi Delta Kappan*, 486-489.

Nanus, B. (1992). *Visionary leadership: Creating a compelling sense of direction for your organization.* San Francisco: Jossey-Bass.

National Association of Secondary School Principals. (1996). *Breaking ranks: Changing an American institution.* Reston, VA: Author.

Newmann, F. M. (1993). Beyond common sense in educational restructuring: The issue of content and linkage. *Educational Researchers, 22*(2), 4-13, 22.

Owens, R. G. (1991). Leadership. In *Organizational behavior in education* (4th ed., pp. 132-142). Englewood Cliffs, NJ: Prentice Hall.

Patterson, J. L., Purkey, S. C., & Parker, J. V. (1986). *Productive school systems for a nonrational world.* Alexandria, VA: Association for Supervision and Curriculum Development.

Peterson, K. (1995). Critical issue: Building a collective vision. Critical issues in professional development (from The pathways to school improvement home page) [On-line]. Available: URL:http://www.ncrel.org/sdrs/areas/issues/educatrs/leadrshp/

Peterson, K. (1996, November). Developing a mission and vision for the school. In *Reform Talk* (Issue No. 6). Comprehensive Regional Assistance Center Consortium-Region VI, University of Wisconsin-Madison: Wisconsin Center for Education Research, School of Education.

Rosenthal, R., & Jacobson, L. (1968). *Pygmalion in the classroom.* New York: Holt, Rinehart & Winston.

Sarason, S. B. (1996). *Revisiting "The culture of the school and the problem of change."* New York: Teachers College Press.

Sashkin, M., & Egermeier, J. (1992). *School change models and processes* (Office of Educational Research and Improvement). Washington, DC: Government Printing Office.

Schein, E. H. (1985). *Organizational culture and leadership.* San Francisco: Jossey-Bass.

Schlechty, P. (1990). *Schools for the 21st century.* San Francisco: Jossey-Bass.

Schmuck, R., & Schmuck, P. (1992). *Small districts, big problems: Making school everybody's house.* Newbury Park, CA: Corwin.

Sergiovanni, T. J. (1990). *Value-added leadership: How to get extraordinary performance in schools.* San Diego, CA: Harcourt Brace Jovanovich.

Sergiovanni, T. J. (1992). *Moral leadership: Getting to the heart of school improvement.* San Francisco: Jossey-Bass.

Sizer, T. R. (1984). *Horace's compromise.* Boston: Houghton Mifflin.

Sizer, T. R. (1992). *Horace's school.* Boston: Houghton Mifflin.

Slavin, R. E. (1989). PET and the pendulum: Faddism in education and how to stop it. *Phi Delta Kappan, 70*(10), 752-758.

SouthEastern Regional Vision for Education. (1994). *Overcoming barriers to school reform in the southeast* (Office of Educational Research and Improvement, U.S. Department of Education Contract No. RP 91002010).

Sparks, D., & Hirsh, S. (1997). *A new vision for staff development*. Alexandria, VA: Association for Supervision and Curriculum Development and National Staff Development Council.

Sparks, D., & Loucks-Horsley, S. (1989). Five models of staff development for teachers. *Journal of Staff Development, 10*(4), 40-57.

Starratt, R. J. (1995). *Leaders with vision*. Thousand Oaks, CA: Corwin.

Swap, S. (1993). *Developing home-school partnerships*. New York: Teachers College Press.

Tewel, K. (1991, October). Promoting change in secondary schools. *NASSP Bulletin, 75*(537), 10-17.

Tewel, K. (1993, May). Moving toward whole school reform: What the principal can do. *NASSP Bulletin, 77*(553), 46-56.

Thelen, H. (1954). *The dynamics of groups at work*. Chicago: University of Chicago Press.

Thelen, H. (1960). *Education and the human quest*. New York: Harper.

Tyack, D. B., & Cuban, L. (1995). *Tinkering toward utopia: A century of public school reform*. Cambridge, MA: Harvard University Press.

Warner, C. (1994). *Promoting your school*. Thousand Oaks, CA: Corwin.

Watkins, K. E., & Marsick, V. J. (1993). *Sculpting the learning organization*. San Francisco: Jossey-Bass.

Wheatley, M. J. (1992). *Leadership and the new science*. San Francisco: Berrett-Koehler.

Wood, C. J. (1984). Participatory decision making: Why doesn't it seem to work? *The Educational Forum, 49*(1), 55-64.

Wood, C. J. (1989). Challenging the assumptions underlying the use of participatory decision-making strategies. *Small Group Behavior, 20*(4), 428-448.

Wood, C. J. (1995). *You can't teach what you don't know . . .* (Summary report for the National Science Foundation). Albuquerque: University of New Mexico, Department of Educational Administration.

Wood, C. J. (1998). Human dimensions of supervision. In G. R. Firth & E. F. Pajak (Eds.), *Handbook of research on school supervision* (pp. 1085-1103). New York: Macmillan.

Yukl, G. (1994). *Leadership in organizations* (3rd ed.). Englewood Cliffs, NJ: Prentice Hall.

CORWIN
PRESS

The Corwin Press logo—a raven striding across an open book—represents the happy union of courage and learning. We are a professional-level publisher of books and journals for K–12 educators, and we are committed to creating and providing resources that embody these qualities. Corwin's motto is "Success for All Learners."